Can You or
Can You Not
Sail Under
the Command
of A Pirate?

Marty Corcoran

Copyright © 2023 Marty Corcoran

Can You or Can You Not Sail Under the Command of a Pirate

All rights reserved.

No part of this publication may be reproduced or transmitted in any form or by any means electronic or mechanical, including photocopy, recording, or any information storage and retrieval system now known or invented, without permission in writing from the publisher, except by a reviewer who wishes to quote brief passages in connection with a review written for inclusion in a magazine, newspaper, or broadcast.

Print ISBN: 979-8-35093-328-4
eBook ISBN: 979-8-35093-329-1

Printed in the United States of America

This book is dedicated to my husband, Dan,
and children Erin, Dawn, Matthew, and Joe who have
"LIVED THE RIDE."

Dan, my one and only love, you have been my greatest cheerleader.
You have cheered me on since the day we met. Anything I thought
of doing you were always by my side convincing me I could do it.
And even after 53 years of marriage you went right along with me to seek
out God's will for our lives. No words can express the love I feel with
your support and love. I can't wait to see what the next 53 years brings.

My dear children, you have been with me through all the process
of transformation. As I look at you and your families
I can see and know without a second doubt that all the pain
and change were worth every second.

TABLE OF CONTENTS

ACKNOWLEDGEMENTS

I have had so much help writing this book. As I try to remember and look to the inception and if I forget to include your name, please know it is not intentional but simply a senior moment where I did not remember your significant contributions; however, your input was just as important as everyone else's.

First to my parents, who shared their personal experiences and how God was always with them in a real way. This example I will always be grateful for. It was the best start in life I could have had.

To Marie E. Welch, my precious aunt who always encouraged me and pointed out my talents and encouraged me to write! And for her unconditional love which prompted me to take risks and not think of failure. She taught me it is not about winning and losing. There is never losing; it is about winning and learning.

To my spiritual parents Ruth and Neil Duff, who gave me all the missing pieces I didn't get as a child. The unconditional love, the confidence I needed to know God, not just know about Him. Helping me realize that God placed me here for a reason. Also, for helping me realize they were there for me no matter what the circumstance and so was God. Also, no matter what I did or didn't do, that unconditional love would always be there.

To Fran Grandcolas Grant, who took on the role of grandmother to our four children. Without you they would have never known what a loving grandmother was nor would I.

To Dave Carter, who identified the dysfunction in our family. And, for pointing my husband and me in the correct direction. Otherwise, the transformation may have never taken place and I doubt our family would be together today. Fifty-three years strong.

To "New Life Now" Ministry with Steve Arterburn and the boys. You supplied my family and me with the tools to keep the transformation going and the courage to not give up.

To Don Hammond, who taught me the real meaning of Christianity and the encouragement to do things I never would have believed were possible for me. For seeing in me gifts and talents I never knew or believed existed. You also set another heading in my life: "When I have to answer to God, I would much rather be guilty of too much grace than not enough." You encouraged me to understand that everyone has a story, and it is important to take time and listen to it.

To Cloud and Townsend Resources, and everyone involved in "Ultimate Leadership," "Townsend Leadership Program," and especially to John Townsend, who was there for Dan and me, offering encouragement and guidance through the darkest parts of our transformation.

To Journey Community Church in La Mesa, California, which through example modeled what a church is really supposed to look like in everything they thought, said, and did. And a special thanks to Ed Nobel, who helped me realize that I wasn't way out in left field. We will always call Journey our home no matter where the Lord sends us.

To Jim and Kim Herrera, who have allowed me to bounce ideas off of them and encouraged me with advice to help me get this book out to the world.

To Nancy Sharp, who had the first read-through and encouraged and prompted me to keep going.

To Marc Hedges, my designer, who really understood my mission and goal and created my logo, website, and book cover. You kept that fire going and provided the vision of possibilities for my company and book in the future. You turned this into a reality instead of just a dream.

To my wonderful editor, David Colbert, who has stuck with me and didn't give up on me. This has been a long haul. And because you didn't give up neither did I. You were that candle in the dark that kept the light burning and gave me hope and encouragement to keep moving forward.

And mostly to Jesus, who has been there with His unconditional love and His presence. You have been there and directed me from the moment of inception of the book to getting this out to Your loved ones. May this bring Your loved ones into a relationship with You. My eternal gratitude and thanks, which will continue throughout eternity.

PROLOGUE

"I'm Captain Jack Sparrow! Savvy?" What is my fascination with Jack Sparrow? The first time I saw Jack Sparrow was on a DVD. It was right before *Pirates of the Caribbean: Dead Man's Chest* was coming out and my husband, Dan, wanted me to go and see the movie with him! For Dan, a movie isn't worth seeing unless you see it on the big screen in the theater; and he has the middle seat in the center of the theater's screen. I had missed *Pirates of the Caribbean: Curse of the Black Pearl* in the theater, and he suggested I see the first movie at home before we went out to see *Pirates of the Caribbean: Dead Man's Chest*. Of course, he had seen the movie in the theater, but he was willing to sacrifice and watch it on TV with me. Dan wanted me to see the movie with him, so he assured me the movie was about relationships. That's a must for me, especially if I have to endure any violence and action adventures. I'll admit a part of me thought that my "beloved" was telling me that just to ensure I watched the movie. Oh, well, I was game. My favorite ride at Disneyland has always been Pirates of the Caribbean, ever since Dan and I first rode it in 1973. Though the ride was a little too thrilly for me at first, I really enjoyed it once I rode it a couple of times. So, we watched the DVD together, and Dan was really telling the truth. The movie is all about relationships. Something was drawing me in. I couldn't wait to see *Pirates of the Caribbean: Dead Man's Chest*.

Captain Jack Sparrow was a "somewhat familiar" character in my life. I seemed to know this fellow, and I liked him. I wanted to hang out with him and get to know him better. There was something more to this guy. That could be a dangerous thing for me, liking him, I mean. What would people say? Especially the people I hang out with. In their circles, I was known as Goody Two Shoes, Snow White, and Angel Girl. Hey, who says I can't act? Only I didn't know at the time I was acting. Maybe I am in the wrong business!

When I announced that I had seen *Pirates of the Caribbean: Curse of the Black Pearl* and that I really identified with this Jack character, it caused all kinds of comments. Some were to my face, but most were behind my back. I mean, that is what good Christians do. Never want to hurt the person's feelings. I was told that movie was not something you should be watching, much less enjoying or condoning. Jack is clearly a sinner who will never mend his ways. We've seen previews, they said: he drinks, he's a real alcoholic, he's gay, he lies, and he cares for no one but himself. The guy is mentally deranged. I didn't quite understand how this could all be known from a preview. (I have a theory on that, too!) Oh well, this group of people wouldn't be the group where I could process all my concerns, ideas, and thoughts that were swirling around in my head, for sure. Nevertheless, there was this draw. Something kept pulling me in. I knew this guy. I felt at home and safe around him. And 90 percent of the time, I knew his next move before he did. Jack was anything but predictable, so why did I know his next move? I tried and tried to think of someone in my past who was like Jack. I racked my brain, but nothing came to me. I saw uncles and my dad with bits and pieces of him, but nothing really big enough to write home about. But I knew this guy. This was really bugging me because I couldn't figure this out. But there was also a big part of him that was secret, hidden from the world, but desperately wanting to be known. I knew that place, too. As far as knowing what that part was like, I wasn't really sure. All I knew was that I had a part of me like that, too.

Well, I was certainly hooked, anxious to see *Pirates of the Caribbean: Dead Man's Chest*, and excited to know that a third movie was already being worked on. After *Dead Man's Chest*, I had a million scenarios running in my head for the third movie. I love doing that. Looking at all the possibilities. I like doing that with people, too. Helping them find and see all the possibilities and then letting them discover a solution.

I was a math major in college. I am a teacher and love working with children of all ages. I have also done quite a bit of pastoral care and have helped people with all kinds of issues. My favorite people are what the world considers outcasts or underdogs. Most call them strange or weird. But really, when I look at them, I don't see that. All I see are people who are different from me, but with unique, wonderful gifts, untapped, waiting to be discovered. Since God created all of us uniquely, isn't that how I should see them? They may be unfamiliar to me, but that's the adventure! I like getting to know them for who they really are! Most people, especially church folk, label them and then stay away. How sad, because they are really missing out. For many years that is what I was taught: stay away! But that teaching didn't come from my early adult years, nor my childhood growing up. My parents, especially my dad, thought everyone was cool. He had no use for people who judged other people. Dan's father was the same way. Unfortunately, both our fathers died in our teenage years, and we had some bad guidance in our early adulthoods.

Jack Sparrow kept invading my thoughts. Was it an attraction to the actor, Johnny Depp? Not really, believe it or not. I didn't really know much about him or who he was. I started with a Google search on him. Looking at his filmography, I found many of his movies were my favorites. However, I had never even realized that the movies had the same actor in them. I'm sure that can be credited to Mr. Depp's excellent acting ability. Now I really felt stupid. I had been watching the same person in all these movies and didn't even know it. I'm also like that with music, I must confess. I listen to the songs because I like the different sounds. They often turn out to be by the same artists. The movies were the same. I liked them for the subject matter and character development that occurred in the films. So my next question was, what did all these movies have in common, besides Johnny Depp? I pondered this for quite some time. I was amazed that there was this common thread: when we look at a person, we immediately draw conclusions without getting to know who the person really is. Our conclusions actually keep us from getting to know the person any better. Nothing is really as it seems. Interestingly, I was about to find out that it was no different for *Pirates of the Caribbean*. The same theme existed. Mr. Depp has the unique ability to take the viewers beyond their pre-drawn conclusions about the character, actually getting them to know the person (the character) for who he really is. Just like Jack kept asking in the movie, "But why is the rum gone?" I kept asking why there was this attraction to the character, Jack? What is it about Jack? I was about to be taken on a journey that would question my very being and character.

I am a mother of four, and our second eldest was expecting. She was living about 400 miles south of me at this time. Her husband was on an overseas hardship tour in the military. The third installment of *Pirates of the Caribbean* was due to come out, and I thought it would be fun to watch the first two movies again. If my memory had served me correctly when the first two movies were released, our daughter had been serving hardship tours herself overseas. So, I brought the DVDs with me when I went for a visit to see her.

As I mentioned, most of my early acquaintances labeled good ole Captain Jack as a drunk, gay, mentally ill (crazy) liar and a thief. I heard this so much that I thought maybe there was something wrong with me because I didn't see Captain Sparrow that way. I was anxious to see my daughter's reaction. She is not one to judge people and always seems to be very objective. In fact, I can say that about all our children.

We watched both movies, and then I asked her, "What is your impression of Captain Jack?" Her response was the inspiration for this book! With a smile on her face and compassion in her heart, she said, "Pretty cool, a pirate with MS."

It was one of those ah-ha moments. People see and label people through their own life's experiences. I have MS and Jack was exhibiting behaviors she'd seen in me. Balance issues, slurred speech, confusion, and a desire to keep pressing on and letting nothing get the best of you. Many people had given me similar labels like Jack's behind my back at different times in my life. What keeps me pressing on? Why am I drawn to this character, Jack Sparrow? What is the attraction to pirates? I invite you to go on this journey with me.

CHAPTER ONE: FAMILIARITY

You Seem Somewhat Familiar…
Does Jesus?

One of my favorite quotes by Dan Eldon (photographer) that I keep in front of me as much as possible is, "The journey is the destination." I believe that life is that journey, and our job is to continue to grow and learn until our life here on earth is finished. I also believe that once we are with our creator we will continue to grow and learn for all eternity.

I was raised in an Irish Catholic family. I was the youngest of four children. My siblings were 22, 16, and 14 when I was born. My mom was an alcoholic and my dad was a compulsive gambler. With that said, there was always a roof over our heads and food on the table. However, neither parent was emotionally present. I learned about Jesus at an early age. He was a household name. My parents shared stories of how He had intervened in their lives. In my inner self, I began feeling His presence and somehow, He filled the void that my parents created. My siblings had all moved out and got married before I was five years old. I experienced a great deal of loneliness. Though I did not see visions or hear voices, I sensed His love for me, reassured by His presence.

I attended Catholic school, beginning my formal training about God, Jesus, the Holy Spirit, Mary, the church, etc. But as I heard some teachings about Jesus, my experience with Him would disagree with their teachings. Inside I would yell, "That's not right! That's not the Jesus I know."

I first read the Bible in my early adult years. I would get sidetracked into listening to others' interpretations and doubting my own. The process would take many years until I would return to my own experiences with Jesus to read the Bible with my own eyes instead of the eyes of others.

I want to share my journey with you, not because your journey should look like mine, but to encourage you to embark on your own journey. Do not be discouraged if it has nothing in common with anyone else's. God created each of us as a unique being. He has a unique plan for each of us. As we begin to experience Him, He will give us insights along the way if we listen to our hearts. God speaks intimately to each of us as we begin to develop our relationship with Him. He desperately wants this relationship with us, one He will pursue until the end of time. If we open our eyes, ears, and hearts, His presence will become obvious to us. What I've come to realize is that in my own life, JESUS IS A PIRATE! Captain Jack was reminding me of Jesus.

Before I scare half the population away, I think it is important that I should define what I mean by *pirate*. Johnny Depp has forever changed the world's image of a pirate. Mr. Depp forces us to look once again past our preconceived notions to the individual. Research about pirates reveals the following:

> Sailors of the 17th and 18th centuries found life at sea hard and dangerous. Seamen were often tricked or kidnapped by naval press gangs into serving on men-of-war, where they were subjected to appalling conditions and harsh discipline. This was called being gang-pressed. Compared to this, a pirate's life offered freedom and easy money, and many pirate crews were made up of formerly honest seamen.
>
> (Platt, Richard, Eyewitness Books *PIRATE*, DK Publishing, Inc. 2007, page 7)

This seems to be a consistent view among several authors. It is even the case for Jack Sparrow. He never wanted to be a pirate. In fact, he was running away from his family, who were pirates. (Kidd, Rob, *Pirates of the Caribbean Jack Sparrow, Sins of the Father* vol. 10, Disney Press, New York, page 5).

> Sparrow can be identified by the pirate brand, "P". Sparrow was marked with this brand by the East India Trading Company's very own Lord Cutler Beckett (God rest his soul) after Sparrow refused to sail the cargo assigned to him by the East India Trading Company. Beckett did not feel that the fact that the cargo was human should be considered. Sparrow was given an order, and he refused to abide by it, instead he released the slaves and set them free. Behavior such as this is proof of Sparrow's wild and erratic nature—and of his piracy.

(Faye, Sir Thomas, *Disney Pirates of the Caribbean, The Secret Files of the East India Trading Company*, Disney Press, New York)

Six Characteristics of a Pirate

Using Beckett's reasoning as a starting point, I've come up with six characteristics of a pirate.

1. A pirate is a person who values freedom above all else.

Jack desperately wanted the *Black Pearl* back because of what it represented. "What a ship is, what the *Black Pearl* really is, is freedom." Freedom is of number one importance to God and Jesus. God sent Jesus to set us free.

> "Christ has set us free to live a free life. So, take your stand! Never again let anyone put a harness of slavery on you."

> (Galatians 5:1, *The Message*)

> "It is absolutely clear that God has called you to a free life. Just make sure that you don't use this freedom as an excuse to do whatever you want to do and destroy your freedom. Rather, use your freedom to

serve one another in love; that's how freedom grows." (Galatians 5:13, *The Message*)

In these two verses, we see just how important freedom is. We were created to be free, and it wasn't until the garden incident that our freedom was taken away. Because we were created to be free, we are always seeking it. But as Galatians 5:13 points out, freedom can be misused. When it is, our freedom is actually destroyed. Many pirates did misuse their freedom, and when they did, they were destroyed. Take the aforementioned incident where Jack was working for Cutler Beckett of the East India Trading Company as Captain of the *Black Pearl*, which was then called the *Wicked Wench*. He was given a large cargo of slaves from Africa to deliver. A misuse of freedom would have been to have the attitude that he, Jack, was free to deliver these slaves so he could be paid. Instead, Jack reasoned that all men should be free, and his freedom was no more valuable than the freedom of the slaves, so he freed them. That decision cost him his job and his ship (which was sunk). Jack was branded a pirate and thrown into prison. But he was still free. He chose to act on his values rather than the values of the society in which he worked. In doing so, he maintained his freedom to choose to do the right thing.

"When we trust in him, we're free to say whatever needs to be said, bold to go wherever we need to go." (Ephesians 3:12, *The Message*)

2. Pirates were the outcasts of society.

Pirates were also those who went against the grain. That is not all bad or all good. Just like everything else, there were good pirates and bad pirates. In studying them, you can understand why they wanted to be different, and society felt they were outcasts. Most outcasts had been mistreated and abused by society. So, they rebelled. When Jesus came to earth, many considered him an outsider. Although Jesus was Jewish, he was still considered an outsider to the Jewish leaders. The crowds that came to listen knew the Romans could come at any minute to break up His speeches and healings. His own disciples questioned what he did at times and were even afraid to be around Him. Jesus was a rebel. He certainly stirred things up. He disturbed the peace. He respected women, treating them as equals to men.

The following story from the Bible is one of my favorites. It made me want to know Jesus more.

"After this he went out and saw a man named Levi at his work collecting taxes. Jesus said, 'Come along with me.' And he did—walked away from everything and went with him.

Levi gave a large dinner at his home for Jesus. Everybody was there, tax men and other disreputable characters as guests at the dinner. The Pharisees and their religious scholars came to his disciples greatly offended. 'What is he doing eating and drinking with crooks and "sinners?"'

Jesus heard about it and spoke up, 'Who needs a doctor: the healthy or the sick? I'm here inviting outsiders, not insiders—an invitation to a changed life, changed inside and out.'

They asked him, 'John's disciples are well-known for keeping fasts and saying prayers. Also, the Pharisees. But you seem to spend most of your time at parties. Why?'

Jesus said, 'When you're celebrating a wedding, you don't skimp on the cake and wine. You feast. Later you may need to pull in your belt, but this isn't the time. As long as the bride and groom are with you, you have a good time. When the groom is gone, the fasting can begin. No one throws cold water on a friendly bonfire. This is Kingdom Come!

'No one cuts up a fine silk scarf to patch old work clothes; you want fabrics that match. And you don't put wine in old, cracked bottles; you get strong, clean bottles for your fresh vintage wine. And no one who has ever tasted fine aged wine prefers un-aged wine.'"

(Luke 5:27–39, *The Message*)

Many times, we as Christians are so busy trying to *look like* a Christian or Christ follower that we forget how to actually be one.

If you read about Jack as a youth, you learn very quickly that he never really wanted to be a pirate. His family members were pirates, and he ran away from them. Over the course of the year after he ran away, he learned from his heart that what's important is not the group we belong to or reject, but who we are as people. That was a lesson that served him well, because when Cutler Beckett branded him a pirate, he didn't change his behavior to go along with what society expected of a pirate. He was content to continue to be Captain Jack Sparrow. And if you pay attention to the movies, you never hear Jack refer to himself as a pirate. When others bring it up, he will finally, although reluctantly, concede that he is a pirate. However, Beckett imposed that label on him by forcibly branding him a pirate. Jack never lets that external label define who he is.

> Jesus addressed this issue in the following verse. Instead of being busy announcing "I am a Christian," I need to concentrate on who God created me to be and what His purpose is for me. "Jesus commented, 'This tax man, not the other, went home made right with God. If you walk around with your nose in the air, you're going to end up flat on your face, but if you're content to be simply yourself, you will become more than yourself.'"
>
> (Luke 18:14, *The Message*)

3. Pirates have no place to call home.

Being outcasts, pirates were always on the run. The British had gang-pressed many, and they were taken from their homeland. Several hoped to get enough money so that someday they could return home, start a family, and build and run a homestead. Because they were hunted by the British, they couldn't stay at any place for any length of time for fear of being found. If they were known to be or suspected of being a pirate, their only fate was hanging by the neck until dead. That's why the sea made sense. It was far more difficult to search the oceans and seas than to search the land. It was also much harder to be surprised by an attacker while on the open ocean. They could see for miles in every direction. There were far more people and many more chances for surprise attacks on land. They would come into a port for only a very short time in order to stock the ship with food, dry goods, lumber, and other supplies, which they needed.

Jesus traveled from place to place staying at the homes of his disciples. Sometimes townspeople would invite him and the disciples in, but at times he lay outside for sleep. So, Jesus was very familiar with not having a home. A Pharisee questioned him about the fact that he didn't have a home. A verse mentioned in two Gospels speaks to the issue: "Jesus replied, 'Foxes have holes and birds of the air have nests, but the Son of Man has no place to lay his head'" (Luke 9:58 New International Version [NIV] 1984) (Matthew 8:20, NIV1984). That he had no physical home didn't seem to bother him at all. He kept asking people to follow him, but he told them what conditions to expect.

I believe Jesus was more concerned about relationships with people because God created us for relationship. We must have it to thrive. Jesus very much understood the cost and sacrifice involved in putting Him first and following Him. He speaks of it both in Matthew and Luke:

"And not only you, but anyone who sacrifices home, family, fields—whatever—because of me, will get it all back a hundred times over, not to mention the considerable bonus of eternal life." (Matthew 19:29, *The Message*)

"'Yes,' said Jesus, 'and you won't regret it. No one who has sacrificed home, spouse, brothers and sisters, parents, children—whatever—will lose out. It will all come back multiplied many times over in your lifetime. And then the bonus of eternal life!'"

(Luke 18:29–30, *The Message*)

As I said, God created us for relationship. Therefore, it is not an option; it is what we need to live and thrive. We can choose whether our relationships are functional and healthy or dysfunctional and unhealthy. If we choose to do it God's way, we will have functional and healthy relationships. It also requires continual work on the relationship by all parties involved.

Jesus comments on the relationships in the following verses.

"Live in me. Make your home in me just as I do in you. In the same way that a branch can't bear grapes by itself but only by being joined to the vine, you can't bear fruit unless you are joined with me." (John 15:4, *The Message*)

"But if you make yourselves at home with me and my words are at home in you, you can be sure that whatever you ask will be listened to and acted upon."

"I've loved you the way my Father has loved me. Make yourselves at home in my love. If you keep my commands, you'll remain intimately at home in my love. That's what I've done—kept my Father's commands and made myself at home in his love."

(John 15:7, 9–10, *The Message*)

Pirates compensated for being treated as outsiders by becoming each other's family. This satisfied the need for relationship and fulfilled the desire to belong. In their case the relationships were dysfunctional and unhealthy in many ways. Jesus and the disciples became each other's family; however, their relationships were healthy and functional. I have read several studies that all agree that if you had had those disciples living together without Jesus, they probably would have killed each other just as the pirates did.

4. Pirates are present to the moment. They are concerned with the here and now.

Usually, a pirate's main concern was what was going on at the moment. They were always dealing with surviving. They were not very concerned with the past or the future, for that matter. This was especially true because they were always being hunted by society to be punished or hanged.

Society considered them a threat. Although Jesus talked about heaven and His Father, he was very much into the here and now. We get so distracted about what we must do in order for certain things to happen in the future that we miss what's actually going on right now in the present. On many occasions, by the time we realize what is happening, the opportunity has already passed for us to respond and further the kingdom. Repent (repent means change, not stop; this is gradual and doesn't happen immediately) from your sins. The Kingdom is here. *Now!*

5. Pirates live by a code.

Pirates were keenly aware of injustices to others. They were constantly being abused themselves. Pirates were at the mercy of the captain and officers of the crew. Remember that in the beginning they had been gang-pressed onto ships to work as lowly sailors. In the beginning all a pirate's salary was used to pay for uniforms that he never asked for. Also, if he wanted any items that the crew took away from him, he had to buy them back.

The captain of the ship made the rules to achieve whatever he wanted. Rules varied from captain to captain and ship to ship. Oftentimes it also depended on the mood of the captain as well. One day the captain could be in a good mood and everything was excused. The next day the smallest infringement could result in being keel-hauled (tied up with rope and dragged under the ship against the sharp barnacles). For this reason, pirates had a set of rules to be followed that were fair to all. A democracy was formed. Some of our own Declaration of Independence was even based on this code. Jesus also lived by a code.

"What is written in the Law?' he asked him. "How do you read it?"

He answered, "Love the Lord your God with all your heart, with all your soul, with all your strength, and with all your mind', and, 'your neighbor as yourself." "You have answered correctly" he told him. "Do this and you will live."

(Luke 10:26–28, Christian Standard Bible [CSB])

In Jesus' case He fulfilled the law and summed it up with two statements. This was the code Jesus lived by and the one He wants us to follow. If you look closely, you will notice that if you obey those two rules you end up obeying all ten commandments.

6. These guys are obsessed with treasure.

When one thinks of pirates one word always comes to mind. Treasure! As Captain Sparrow so aptly put it, "Not all treasure is silver and gold, mate." But like any treasure you must find it and you can't find it if you're not looking for it. You can't enjoy it if you bury it. Jesus said the kingdom (treasure) is here now so why not act like it? Why not look for it? Why not share it?

> The kingdom of heaven is like **treasure**, buried in a field, that a man found and reburied. Then in his joy he goes and sells everything he has and buys that field.

> (Matt. 13:44, CSB)

CHAPTER TWO: BEATING THE DEVIL

Even Jack Sparrow Can't Best the Devil;
Jesus Can and Does

Jack certainly seems to understand things happen in life that we have no control over. We can either try and change that which we can't, or we can get on with life. However, many people never grasp this concept. This is the place where Christians easily get stuck and never go further in their spiritual growth! Simply put, these are Christians who believe Christ died for their sins, so it is all settled. They won't go to hell. If they can pass this message on to as many as possible and those people do the same, the gates of heaven will be overflowing. Well, between you and me, that's not much incentive for me to be a Christian.

When people see Jack for the first time or have heard of him all they do is tell you he is a despicable *pirate*! Nothing is mentioned of the good that he has done for others. Only part of his story is being told. When people say if you don't believe that Jesus is your savior and don't get baptized you are going to hell, I believe they are telling only a part and misrepresented story of Jesus. Then they encourage you to go out and share this story so their church will grow. They are mystified when it doesn't.

As I pondered this dilemma, I did some research and studying. I came to realize that we are only telling part of the story of Jesus. Not only are we telling just part of the story, but we are also missing the boat, so to speak. We leave all the good stuff out.

Fear is the opposite of love and God is love. Why would we want anyone to come to God because they are afraid of Him and afraid of Hell? No wonder the church seems to be dying, and people are searching elsewhere for something to fill the void in their lives. I think when we are confused about things, it is always best to start at the beginning. Not on page 3 of the Bible (the fall) but on page 1 (the creation). So, if you will bear with me, I would like to start at the beginning and tell you the story as I understand it.

When God created, it was GOOD. The first thing he created was light. The light he separated from the darkness. Try to picture in your mind what God created and what man created. Now visualize everything without man's creation. I believe the light was so we could see God's creation. He separates land and water. We have mountains, streams, vegetation, deserts, plains, oceans, cliffs, jungles, rain forests, everything provided for nature and creatures to survive. Man hasn't even shown up on the scene yet. There are some who can place themselves in a situation like this and totally feel God's presence. All these surroundings are an expression of God himself. Even in the darkness He is there.

In the prologue of this book I referred to my daughter who served in the military. She happened to be stationed at Twentynine Palms, California. Trust me when I say twenty-nine is being very generous. There is no reason to go there unless you are in the military. At this time her unit happened to be doing a nighttime exercise. Since her car had broken down, I volunteered to take her out and drop her off knowing she'd get a ride back the following week when the exercise was over. I have never been in a darker place in my life. No lights at night. The black was the darkest I had ever seen when I parked and turned off my headlights. She held my hand and walked me to a tent. She had the steps memorized like a blind person. I set the stuff down that I helped her carry then asked if this was where she slept. She said, "No, come with me and I'll show you." We walked a bit and then she said to sit down, then to lie down on a sleeping bag on the ground. I couldn't breathe. Looking up I felt I could reach out and touch stars. Literally in front of my face were millions of them all over the sky. All around. Had I not looked up, I would have only seen darkness. Instead, I saw beauty, His beauty. Astronomy maps at Twentynine Palms are sold by the caseloads to the soldiers, Marines, etc. They love to discover what they are seeing. Every time they come back the earth has turned, and the constellations are different. It's hard to sleep with all that beauty. I didn't want to return to the car and drive home. Of course, I didn't have a choice. It wasn't as dark going back. I was so aware God was there. That made all the difference.

I understand that God wants to share all his creation with us. He gave us a similar urge. Think about it. Even as children, when we create, we must share it with someone—a teacher, a friend, a parent. God created us to share with others.

Think about Jack; he is always around people. He says he wants to just be alone but even when he has the chance, he is always getting involved in someone's life. When we were created, we were created for relationship. According to Genesis, Chapter 2, Adam had a great relationship with God. They walked through the garden and talked. Adam named the animals, and God watched. God realized and stated that it was not good for man to be alone. No matter how good we are, we can't relate totally to our creator. There are just some things we can't understand. After all, He is God. The good news is that because He is God and because He created us, He totally understands us. Man needed someone on his own level he could relate to.

So, God created Eve. Now Adam not only had someone who totally understood him, but he had someone he could totally understand. But just like God and Adam worked on their relationship, Adam and Eve had to work on their relationship. And so it is today with our relationships.

Adam and Eve had everything they needed, but Satan had to enter the picture and sprinkle a little doubt around. Thus, the break in the relationships started. Instead of talking to God about their frustration at not being able to understand everything about God, Eve talked with Satan about it. Much like we do in our relationships they added a third party into the mix. We call this triangulation. More doubt develops. Now she was convinced God was keeping something good from her and Adam. All she had to do was eat the forbidden fruit of the tree of Knowledge of Good and Evil to know the truth, or so she thought.

She eats of the tree and then turns to Adam, who shares in her bad decision. God was like any good parent, you know. When your kid screws up you have this gut feeling to go and help them. But a good parent doesn't just rescue, they play the movie forward to see what needs to be done so the child doesn't get trapped again. God came looking for Adam and Eve and modeled how this parenting should work. Unfortunately, Adam and Eve now had the desire to judge good from evil and quickly came to the conclusion that they had screwed up, and they wanted to hide because they felt ashamed.

They obviously didn't get what they hoped for when eating the fruit, because they still didn't understand God or know everything. When God found them and asked them where they were, they were hiding (I think by His question there is still time to patch things up).

Have you ever argued a point until you realized what you said no longer mattered? It is time for action. Jack is a man who never seems to argue. He says his piece and is quiet. This would be the point where we would stop wasting time, walk away, and save it for someone who cares. That's the difference. You see God loves Adam and Eve. No matter what happens, He is not going to give up on them.

When they finally admitted they were hiding because they were so ashamed blame started going around. Adam blamed Eve, and Eve blamed the serpent. I believe if they had owned up to what they had done God would have forgiven them. However, since no one would take ownership of the misdeed, God played the movie forward and decided it was time to take action. There was another tree there in the center of the garden, the tree of eternal life. God knew He had to save Adam and Eve from themselves. He loved them too much to let them self-destruct and be without their relationship with Him. So, He threw them out of the garden, posted angels as guards to keep them out, and not let them touch the tree of eternal life while they were estranged from Him. If He allowed them access to the tree and they went to it, it would have meant they would be eternally separated from Him. He could not bear that even if the pair did not realize why God did what He did.

But God couldn't just leave Adam and Eve to themselves. Though He would try and relate, they just wouldn't get it. As humans, we simply can't fathom or totally understand God; we just can't conceive what was so terrible about what Adam and Eve did. Oh, we give the simple answer they disobeyed God. Well, between you and me, I am sure I could cite numerous times I have disobeyed God. Many times, it was unintentional, but I still disobeyed.

Just like Adam could relate to Eve and totally understand her and she could understand him, God would need to reach down and be on man's level so we could relate and understand. God decided to send His Son because all of us have been on one or both sides of a parent–child relationship. God had great plans for man, and still does, but because the relationship was broken man was now responsible for doing things he wasn't created or designed to do. God would have to go about the implementation of His original plans a little differently. In fact, I wouldn't be at all surprised if He put His plans on hold to get this relationship problem back on track worldwide before we moved on with His original plans.

Jesus would be our model. He would deal with every challenge we could face and show us how to deal with the issues involving God in the relationship instead of running and hiding. There is a great survey put out by Princeton University. Being a teacher, I refer to it often. It seems to me that God is in agreement with it. It states:

PEOPLE REMEMBER

- 10 percent of what is read (Scripture reading)
- 20 percent of what is heard (listening to others)
- 30 percent of what is seen (life observations)
- 50 percent of what is seen and heard (observing what others say)
- 70 percent of what is said (verbalized or translated like Jesus did in the parables)
- 90 percent of what is said and done (modeled like Jesus did)

The comments in parentheses are my own.

Now that we have Jesus as a model for us, we still have one other issue to address. That issue is the consequence of eating from the tree of the Knowledge of Good and Evil. So, we always have this judgment thing going on. We have to decide wrong and right, and we have the eye-for-an-eye and the tooth-for-a-tooth mentality. No matter how hard we try, we can never be good enough. Only God is perfect.

God knew that we could not be about His business with this guilt and judgment hanging over our heads. We were never created or designed to judge. That would be like man flying unassisted. History tells us we're excellent fallers but poor fliers.

God decided to fix this for us. His Son's sacrifice would be payment in full for us all. To seal the deal, He resurrected Jesus from the dead, to prove Jesus was indeed God. Once you can grasp and accept that, you can have a clean slate with God and be ready to go about His business.

We must always use Jesus as our model in all we think, say, and do. We really have to own Jesus' passions and desires, and let our hearts be broken when His is broken. It will take a lifetime to get there, but that is the purpose of our journey.

Let's look at Jack for a minute. He was born into piracy. As a child he ran away from it. As a young adult he was really tested when he was asked to deliver the slaves to America from Africa. Instead, he set the slaves free. This was definitely the opposite of an act of piracy, but he was branded a pirate because of that very act and was thrown into prison. He would spend the rest of his life trying to do the right thing but to most of the British he would always be a pirate. Why? Because they refused to get to know him as a person and have a relationship with him.

There was one other character in the garden we have yet to talk about. That would be Lucifer or Satan. The crucifixion and resurrection settled this battle *forever*.

Satan always wanted to be God or better than God. Unable to achieve this aim, he spends his time trying to get *us* to want to be God or better than God. The good news is, once we choose a relationship with God, the deal is sealed, and Satan can't win us over. Jesus won, there is no turning back. No undoing. But God gave us free will when He created us, and He will not take it away. We have to choose which path we want. If you choose to stay away or not deal with the issues, God will pursue you until the day you die. He will never take your choice away. In POTC3, Elizabeth Swan, Will's love, told James Norrington, the British Naval Officer and Jack's childhood friend, "Know what side you choose!"

When we think of Satan, we usually associate the word "evil" with him. The word is fire breathing and ugly. But I heard a different definition of evil which I think fits much better. It was from the CBS Television show *Joan of Arcadia*.

"No, evil is not ugly and fire breathing; it is charming and beautiful. It makes you doubt yourself with one small compromise after another until it whittles you down, and it functions best when no one believes in it."

Isn't that what Satan did to Eve? Create doubt?

Satan is smart, charming, and cunning. But he is the enemy. There is a great quote from the movie *Pearl Harbor*, which states, "The smart enemy hits you exactly where you think you are safe." Where do you feel safe today?

The battle is over, the war is won. As for me, I'm choosing the winning side.

CHAPTER THREE:
LEGACY

"But Pirate's in Your Blood Boy,
So You'll Have to Square with That Someday!" (POTC1)
Have You?

I was flying back home to San Jose after visiting my grandchildren in Ohio. Because my four children live all over the U.S., it is unusual to get to see all my grandchildren and children in one location. I had thoroughly enjoyed my visit and was a little worn out keeping up with three grandchildren age six and under. It was the second and final leg of the six-hour journey and the plane was packed. I always prefer aisle seats, but had a window seat this time. It was a large plane, seating six in each row with an aisle down the center. There was only one empty seat on the plane and that happened to be the middle seat in my row. The woman sitting next to me and I were hoping it didn't get filled. Then we both could stretch out a little for the five-hour flight ahead. The stewardess was just about ready to shut the door when we heard a deep commanding voice call out to hold on. Then a man in his late 40s or early 50s appeared at the front of the plane and headed for our empty seat. He was scruffy looking with a mustache and scraggly beard, both matching his sun-bleached hair, which was curly, semi-long, and looked like it hadn't been combed for days. He had deep tanned skin and an earring in his left ear. He was wearing jean shorts, flip flops, and a half unbuttoned plaid shirt. As he approached us, you could see as he bounced down the aisle that he was on the cell phone. He talked in a loud commanding voice, but there was a certain kindness in how he spoke. He then said, "This is Captain Davis. I am now on the plane to San Jose. Transfer all calls now to–" (some seven-digit number). "I will log in when I get to San Jose." He then closed the cell phone and put it in his pocket.

When I heard him say "Captain," my ears immediately perked up, being the wife of a former army officer and the mother of a Marine. Something didn't track. His looks definitely told me he wasn't military unless he was undercover. So, my next guess was that he was a sea captain. Time would tell. As he approached, he eyed the empty seat. I don't think he had bathed in a few days from the smell, but he had a great smile and eyes that danced and sparkled as he looked at and engaged with people. When my husband and I meet people like this, we always use the phrase, "There was somebody home." There was definitely someone home here. You could tell he loved people.

He swayed a little and then plopped down in the seat. As his eyes met mine and his lips turned up to say hello, I realized, *Oh my goodness, he is a modern day Jack Sparrow.* I was certainly going to enjoy this trip, and as I got to know Captain Martin Davis over time, he proved my suspicions right. Captain Davis was a merchant seaman. He had joined the U.S. Merchant Marine during the Vietnam war. After he served in Vietnam and came back home, he decided to go back to school. He worked hard and got a Ph.D., but still felt a void in his life. He missed the sea. Said he had to sail. He didn't realize it when he first joined the U.S. Merchant Marine, but he now knew sailing was in his blood and he had to accept that. Or, as Captain Jack says, "He'd have to square with that."

His family thought him crazy, especially his father. He had a Ph.D. and he wanted to be a sailor. He also had a wife and daughter. When he decided to go back to the life he once had, his marriage didn't last, but he and his ex-wife had remained very good friends. She was one of the few who understood him and had done a fine job in bringing up their daughter, and now his daughter was ready to go to college. Captain Davis was still a major part of her life. As he talked about his daughter, his eyes danced and sparkled. His whole face was lit up and animated. I could tell she was the love of his life.

Since we had lots of time and I was intrigued by this gentleman, I asked the good captain where his ship was and why he had taken to flying in planes. I knew there was a simple answer, but I also knew that by asking the question the way I did, I was going to hear the whole grand adventure. I was not disappointed. He was a captain of a cargo ship in the Caribbean, and he had just sailed his cargo ship through Hurricane Gustav. That particular hurricane was expected to cause quite a bit of havoc once it hit the Florida coast in a few days. It was already a Category 4 and gaining strength every day. He described what it was like sailing through that hurricane in 35-foot-high waves and what his crew had had to endure. You could tell he was very close to his crew and knew each man personally and cared for them like they were his own children. He took that responsibility very seriously. That was certainly confirmed when he told me what happened next.

One of Captain Davis's crew members was thrown overboard by a wave that swept over the deck. Davis jumped in to save him and managed to reach him. He had a firm hold on the crew member and was attempting to swim back to the ship. The rough, tumultuous water tore the crew member right out of the captain's arms. The captain was unable to reach his mate and his friend drowned. Captain Davis had just returned from Santa Domingo, where he had had to break the news to the man's wife and four children. He was coming home to Santa Cruz to regroup, rethink, and to be cared for by others so he would be able to give his crew his all when he returned to his ship. He had sailed with that man for ten years. As tears filled the captain's eyes, I felt the great loss this man must be experiencing. All I could manage to say was that I was deeply sorry. As we sat quietly for several minutes, I knew this man didn't take his job lightly. He felt total responsibility. There was no blaming anyone else or the hurricane. I had great respect for Captain Davis. He was doing what he loved, but he accepted the reality of hardship and pain that could come along with it.

I think many times when we choose to follow Jesus, we are under the misconception that everything will be fine now, and life will be grand. That was never promised to us, unfortunately. What *was* promised is that Jesus will walk alongside us, and we will never be alone. The good captain here understood that. He also understood that God uses people to help us. He knew that he could not go it alone and before he could return to his work, the work he was created to do, he must be refilled. He was returning to Santa Cruz to ensure that that would take place.

It is imperative that we all have a group of people that is safe and is there for us (and we for them), where we can be our true selves and be accepted, a group where we receive grace and truth over time.

A group is also a wonderful place to explore and find out where our true gifts and talents lie. Find out what's in your blood so you too can square with that! We can also find out where our talents don't lie and find out where our weaknesses are.

We may not all have the ability to create or participate in a group where we can all be physically together, but we have needs to be met in order to live a healthy and productive life. In his book, *People Fuel*, Pages 80-81, John Townsend describes us as having 22 relational needs. They are:

Be Present
1. Comfort
2. Validation
3. Identification
4. Containment
5. Acceptance
6. Attunement

Convey the Good

7. Affirmation

8. Encouragement

9. Respect

10. Hope

11. Forgiveness

12. Celebration

Provide Reality

13. Clarification

14. Perspective

15. Insight

16. Feedback

17. Confrontation

Call to Action

18. Advice

19. Structure

20. Challenge

21. Development

22. Service

Without these needs being met, we become like someone with a vitamin deficiency. Think about these needs for yourself. What needs are being met and what needs are your vitamin deficiencies? Find a group of people (3+) where you can meet all these needs for each other. In Chapter 5 we will talk about finding those people.

CHAPTER FOUR:
KEEP TO THE CODE

What Code Do Jesus' Followers Have to Follow?

The problem with keeping to the code is understanding exactly what it says. We are really good about putting our own spin on it. However, to truly be able to keep to the code, we have to understand what was going on at the time it was written, and what was the point and purpose of the author who wrote it. Beware of someone who proclaims to know what it all means. Even in the third installment, Captain Teague, who was the keeper of the original Pirate Code, didn't settle the dispute by reciting the code from memory, but by reading what the original code said. *Always* go back and check for yourselves what the Bible says. When someone tells you the Bible says something, check it out. Don't take their word for it. This includes the things that pastors say. Be like the Bereans: "Now the Bereans were of more noble character than the Thessalonians, for they received the message with great eagerness and examined the Scriptures every day to see if what Paul said was true" (Acts 17:11, NIV1984).

This was modeled in the movie. Captain Teague finds the passage that Barbosa was referring to, "An act of war, and this be truly that, can only be declared by a pirate king. And there hasn't been a king since...." Captain Teague looks up the reference and declares that "Barbosa is right." Jack takes a huge RISK here and pushes Captain Teague out of the way and declares, "Wait a minute! Let me see that!" At that moment, you don't know if Teague is going to knock him across the room, shoot him, or let him see for himself. I am sure Jack wasn't 100 percent sure either. If you read *Pirates of the Caribbean: The Original Adventures of Young Jack Sparrow*, Book 10, *Sins of the Father*, you can get a little flavor of the relationship between the two. Captain Teague is Jack's supposed father. Even Jack doesn't know for sure. However, he was the only father figure Jack knew. Most of these growing up years were in a very dysfunctional family. The family, pirates all, was always screaming, yelling, and abusing one another. In fact, Jack's grandmamma tried to kill Jack several times. Captain Teague declares that is her way of showing love. Jack was very cautious of Captain Teague even though he had bailed Jack out of a few dangerous situations. When Jack was 16 and he couldn't take the dysfunction of his family anymore, he ran away from home hoping never to see another pirate or them again.

For anyone who has experienced a relationship like that between Captain Teague and Jack, you know the safest approach is to stay invisible. You keep your mouth shut, and you never rock the boat. When Captain Teague is called inside by Barbosa you realize that this was Jack's approach as well. When Teague says, "You're in my way, boy!" Jack, one of the nine pirate lords, just slides out of the way, right back into that role of his childhood. It is funny how many of us do this in our own family and relationships without even realizing it.

I grew up in an alcoholic family where three unspoken rules reigned:

1. Don't tell anybody.

2. Don't trust anyone.

3. Don't feel anything (emotions).

Even with extensive therapy and work, I always keep a check on the unspoken rules. They will always be with me.

We need to be like Jack when he asks for verification of what Teague reads. We need to dig into what people are telling us about what the Bible says and means. Read it, research it, and research the research. Most importantly, talk to God about it. Be honest when you don't understand something. Ask God to show you. Then wait and watch! God will go out of His way to explain it. But don't limit where you think the answer will be. He uses books, media, songs, movies, movie characters, the people around you, and situations in your life. He will give it to you in several ways. You just keep your question in the forefront and watch for the answer.

If the creator of the universe wrote you a letter, wouldn't you want to know what He's telling you? It says different things to different people at different times in their process of growing toward the Lord. Unfortunately, we look at it as a form letter that everybody received. When we have a question, we ask the next guy what the letter says because he received the same letter. Let's face it. Half the time we can't even find the letter. It's buried with everything else we get in the mail. There will be some who frame it to show it off to all their acquaintances. That makes them feel important.

Where the letter really belongs is in your heart, where no one can take it away. What are you willing to do to get it there? How is that going to happen?

This is the code you need to be safe. Jesus fixed the problem when He reduced the entire code to two statements.

Jesus said, "Love the Lord your God with all your passion and prayer and intelligence." This is the most important, the first on any list. But there is a second to set alongside it: "Love others as well as you love yourself." These two commands are pegs; everything in God's Law and the Prophets hangs from them.

(Matthew 22:37, *The Message*)

What does it mean to love someone? Love is a choice, not a feeling. Love is wanting what is best for the other person. Love is providing a safe haven for that person. Love is helping that person be all that God wants them to be.

However, we usually want people to act in the way that is most convenient to us at the time. We need to remember before we say or do something to play the movie to the end. How is this going to help this person and myself be all we can be?

CHAPTER FIVE:
CLARITY

Not Sunset, Sundown!
Are you reading the Bible through a clear lens?

So, you ask, how does one get it in their heart? First, you must discover the condition of the lens you use to read the Bible.

If you remember in the third installment of *Pirates of the Caribbean*, after the crew had rescued Jack, they were trying to figure out how to get back to the real world. All the crew had access to the chart. All had looked at it and read it. Yet, no one had an answer much less any suggestions. Jack, however, didn't give up. He kept reading and re-reading the map and chart. It wasn't until he started to listen to his heart, deciding what he truly wanted, when he recognized the answer on the map. "Not sunset. Sundown and rise up," he proclaims. He then proceeds to show by example what the crew needs to do. He never tells them what to do.

When we read the Bible, we must ponder and search our hearts. Remember, it is your personal letter from God, and he knows what's in your heart even if you don't.

One Bible book you can do this quite easily with is Proverbs. There are 31 chapters in Proverbs and 30–31 days of each month. If you begin in February, you'll have to read into the first three days of March. Pick the chapter number that corresponds with the day of the month and let the words sink in.

We have all looked at our horoscopes in a newspaper or freed a fortune from a cookie. First, we read them, then we search our hearts to see how they fit and if they apply to what is happening in our life. So, do the same thing in the proverbs you read for the day. It is amazing how God will speak to you!

For over ten years now, I have read the proverbs of the day. Even though I am re-reading the text, I always glean something new. God is a living, breathing God, and His work is alive, too. God is working in our lives. Have you ever wondered how two children can grow up in the same house and yet be totally different? Think about it.

Fogging the Lens

A way to think about this is that when we were born, we had a clear lens (grid) that we looked through to see the world. It was a perfect lens (grid), and when we looked through it, we saw things and experienced things as God did. But we are born into a world of imperfection. So very quickly the lens (grid) changed.

Below is a visual of the perfect lens (grid).

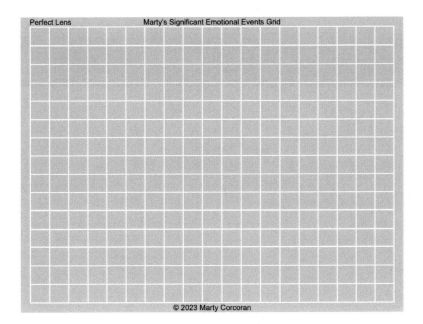

Perfect Lens

The grid lines are invisible (they are shown here so we have a sense of time). Looking at the perfect grid, we saw a clear view, just as God does.

But change happens. Many doctors say that being born is the hardest thing the human body ever goes through. Just after the trauma of birth, the doctor starts prodding and poking, making sure the baby is okay. Pushing a syringe into the baby's nose, the nurse or doctor suctions mucus. Medical staff perform Apgar and PKU tests to grade the baby's responsiveness and reflexes. Some babies are given an hour or so to bond with their mother; while others are whisked away to the nursery to get cleaned up.

Babies are people first and foremost. They are made in God's image (*Imago Dei*) and, though they can't identify their feelings yet, they certainly have them. It is the duty of the parent/guardian to help the baby identify the feelings and help the baby process and metabolize them in a healthy way.

Let's look at a section of the lens (grid) right after the baby has been poked in its heel with a needle for a PKU test.

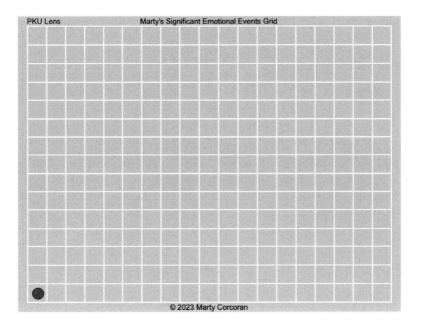

© 2023 Marty Corcoran

PKU Lens

The circles on the lens (grid) represent the different feelings the baby is experiencing. Chances are the baby is going to scream. WHY? Because the baby feels PAIN from the needle! A baby's pains aren't localized: they feel pain all over. If the baby is comforted, the lens (grid) will then look like this.

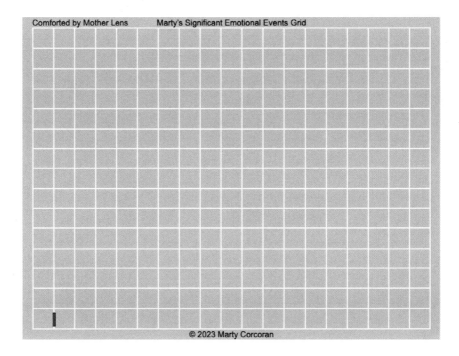

© 2023 Marty Corcoran

Comforted by Mother Lens

Notice the feeling no longer blocks the view of the lens (grid) because it has been processed with the help of the mother. However, if the mother does not help the baby process the feeling, then the lens will look like it did initially when the PKU was administered. So as the baby looks out of the lens, his/her view is blocked.

Our first task is to figure out what our lens looks like. This is another area where many of our churches go wrong in their zeal to grow; they don't tend to the health of the congregation they have.

Did you know that a seaman in the military can be court martialed if he or she gets sunburned? That is because in order to sail a ship you need to be in the best health you can possibly be in. Do you know a military pilot cannot take as much as an Aspirin without consulting his or her assigned doctor? If you have a family history of migraine headaches, you cannot fly at all. The work that our military does is extremely important. Sailing a ship is extremely important. You are responsible for the lives of many other people. If you are not in your best possible health, you are putting the people you are responsible for at a much greater and unnecessary risk.

It seems to me if we are supposed to be about the business of "sharing this good news with others, and helping them," we need to be in the best possible health we can be in both medically and emotionally. Otherwise, we are putting others at a greater and unnecessary risk.

So, the real task here is to figure out exactly what is on our lens. Seems like Jack's lens was pretty foggy. Remember when he was in Davy Jones's Locker? (POTC3) So many Jacks are running around. Each Jack represents a different part of Jack that hasn't been dealt with. So think of each Jack as a big circle on Jack's lens. There was a fearful Jack. An angry Jack. A playful Jack. Each person's lens looks different. Some of our lenses are so filled with circles that we can't possibly see what is really on the other side of that lens.

If your lens looks like one of the two below, you will need some professional help in processing and clearing your grid. Notice that no feelings have been processed.

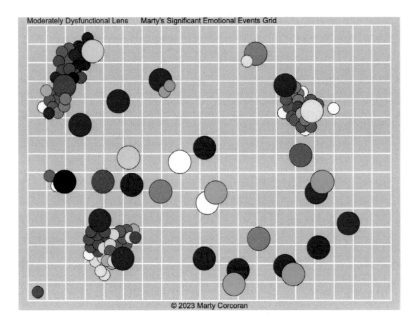

Moderately Dysfunctional Lens

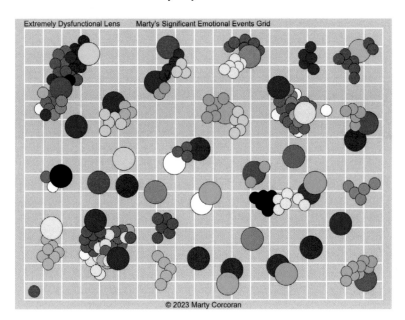

Extremely Dysfunctional Lens

How was Jack able to figure out what the map was really saying? I believe it is because he was looking through a clearer lens. He had just been in Davy Jones's Locker, where he was confronted with his real selves or as I like to call them parts (of himself). He was in the process of integrating all of these parts into one. This is what is known as transformation.

Clearing the Lens

When he could use all of his experiences (i.e., the experience of going "down" to Davy Jones's Locker, POTC3), his life was turned upside down in a sense to right itself. It was like he had to accept who he was and his past experiences and not ignore them. Take what he learned from them and make that a part of him and own it and use it for good. So, he came to the conclusion, "Not sunset but sundown! If I had to go upside down to make it right so does this ship." So, he began to make it happen. He didn't tell anyone else what to do He just did it. It's what I call changing the dance step. Eventually if the people in your life want to keep a relationship with you, they also will follow suit. Notice when he first started going back and forth, they all looked at him like he was crazy. Jack changed the dance step. He still did the same dance just differently. If he would have started acting like the pirate actor Errol Flynn, I think they all would have left him in the locker. It is a process that happens to us one small step at a time. Over time we will notice we do certain things and react in certain ways and think "I wouldn't have done it like this before!"

When our family first moved to Michigan, I began to question whether or not our marriage was in trouble. We had just started going to a church and I really related to the pastor's sermons. But it was a very legalistic type of church. I tried to make an appointment with the pastor and was told that for family issues I should see another pastor who was in charge of that area. I did not even know this pastor, much less what he looked like, but I made an appointment.

Let me just say God was watching over me because I had no idea what I was doing. When I arrived at my appointment, I described an incident between my husband and myself in less than a minute and a half. The pastoral counselor looked at me and said, "You both come from alcoholic homes growing up, and in both cases, it was your mother."

My jaw must have dropped down to the floor. He was absolutely right. But how did he know? He gave me a card and told me he wanted my husband and I to go to this man and woman for counseling. I asked if they were Christian. He asked me if I had a massive heart attack would I want the best heart surgeon or a Christian doctor? Before I could answer, he told me the counselors were specialists in adult children of alcoholics.

The pastoral counselor was only allowed 10 sessions of 30 minutes each to counsel parishioners. We would need far more counseling than that to clear the lens. Little did I know! He said we could use the sessions with him to discuss anything we felt we were being misguided in. The issue never came up in 15 years.

As I was leaving that day, that pastor took me out to the sanctuary and put his hand on my shoulder and said, "See those seats (pews)? They hold about 1,200 people and we have three services each Sunday. Eighty-five percent of all the people sitting in those seats need to go to therapy. It takes real courage to do what you are going to do and if you see it through, God will use you in a powerful way."

Six months later, he was asked to leave that church for his non-legalistic approach. He did. God had his next assignment waiting for him. God still uses him today more strongly than ever.

My point here is, don't just seek out a "Christian counselor" recommended by the church you are attending. Find specialists in any fields you need help with. Research tells us we usually pick a church that matches our dysfunctions (*Secrets of Your Family Tree* by Dave Carder, Earl Henslin, John Townsend, Henry Cloud and Alice Brawand, Page 131. Do your research. It takes a lot of courage to ask for help, but you will never regret it once you can see clearly through your lens.

Perhaps your lens is not full of circles but has some blind spots. There are people that help with that, too. What you don't want to do is go back to the source and try to relive the past. If that worked, you'd have already done it. What needs to be done is to create a new past. This is where these people help. They help you process and get what you need and deserve and never got.

It happens slowly and not all at once. Many times, you don't even realize it has occurred. You just form new honest relationships with safe people. Relationships built on truth and trust. And over time it happens. That's not to say it will all be pleasant or happy, but your friends will be there to see you through that, too! Look at Jack in the first instalment of *Pirates of the Caribbean* and then in the fifth. He certainly is not the same Jack. He has changed over time. One might say he is not the center of the show anymore. He's gotten older and wiser. He thinks and observes a lot more.

Let me make a side comment here. Many people want to be angry with God and ask, "Where was HE?" That is perfectly okay. He can handle it. He knows you are feeling that way. He is just as angry as you are about what happened to you. The people that did this also had free will, unfortunately. But know this: He was right there with you feeling everything you felt and is there right now as you read this wanting you to get the help you need.

Below is an Emotionally Healthy Lens.

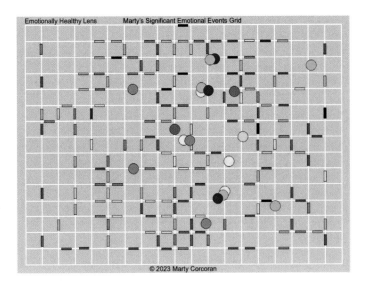

Emotionally Healthy Lens

42

Once you can pretty much see through your lens, make regular appointments with your community. Have your life group, home group, small group (whatever you have named it) around you and meet at least once a week. Then as you support each other, and as you transform your lens, it becomes clearer and you begin seeing thing as God sees things. Our second step is to make sure we are seeing things through our own lens and NOT someone else's. Many times, others like to interpret for us. Be like the Bereans, as Paul says (Acts 17:10-11, NIV1984). Do your own research and don't go to church or listen to a radio or TV broadcast just to have someone interpret for you. Chew up the meat and spit out the bones. Take it to God in prayer and ask, "Help me to know what this really means!" Then by the Holy Spirit using the Bible, prayer, circumstances, and people, God will speak to you. Remember you must pray first about it.

Below is Jesus' lens.

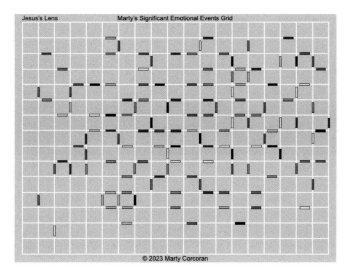

Jesus's Lens

Jesus modeled for us what we are to be doing. Jesus had a safe group of 12 disciples. This is the lens of a sinless person which is always what we are striving for but will never achieve completely this side of heaven.

Notice Jesus' lens. He has processed all the feelings. He experienced every feeling there is. There is no feeling you have that He didn't experience. He processed them with His family, His disciples, His Heavenly Father, and the Holy Spirit. He sees clearly, the way the Father made Him to see. In addition to processing our feelings with God, it is also essential that we process them with our family (if safe), safe friends, and counselors (when appropriate).

CHAPTER SIX:
VERACITY

Norrington: "You actually were telling the truth."
Jack Sparrow: "I do that quite a lot,
yet people are always surprised!" (POTC1)
Are You?

Assumptions. We all make them, based on what we think we know or what we are told others know. Having a husband in the army, I learned the mantra the military has had since time immemorial. They have a saying, "When you assume (ass-u-me), you make an ass out of you and out of me." Throughout most of my life experiences I have found this is true.

Lieutenant Norrington, though in the military, had obviously not heard this little saying. He assumed that nothing Jack said could possibly be the truth. He assumed Jack was only interested in what he wanted and would use his words, no matter how they affected others, to get what he wanted. All these assumptions were based on what was on his grid. Sometimes we do the same thing with the Bible. I read it and assumed I knew what it was saying based on what I had been taught growing up, what other well-meaning Christians were telling me, and what was on my grid.

When I was growing up, anger was never allowed from children. No child growing up in my house would get angry for fear of being punished.

Anger was considered disrespectful. A child should have no reason to be angry at; they simply did what they were told. Because of that "training," I learned to push the feeling of anger so far down inside of me that I didn't realize I had any anger. When other people would get angry, I became very fearful that they would get into trouble. I'd discourage their anger and find ways to make them happy. I'd try to make everyone happy. By doing this I was living a lie. I wasn't telling the truth at all. I actually went through quite a lot of therapy for this and had to rediscover myself.

So, as I read the Bible and interacted with people, I interpreted them through my own lens. This is exactly what James Norrington did with Jack. James and Jack both had very dysfunctional pasts. However, as you read *Sins of the Father*, by Rob Kidd, page 121 you learn that when James was six and Jack was sixteen, James's father, Admiral James Norrington, had captured Jack and Captain Teague. While Captain Teague and Jack were trying to escape, little James was in danger of falling off the ship. Jack became aware of this and tried to get to little James to keep him from falling. Jack was unable to get to James to keep him from falling. Unable to reach him in time, James fell overboard, and Captain Teague jumped in and rescued him. Admiral Norrington yelled and told little James he was a disgrace to the Norrington family and it would have been better for him to drown than to be rescued by a pirate. If James wanted to be accepted by the British upper class, he certainly could have nothing to do with Jack. James's lens was cloudy. He certainly couldn't see clearly.

When I read the Bible, I clung to all the verses that said anything negative about anger. I also slid by or never even saw the ones that supported anger. I was totally seeing things out of context. Or another way to put it, I was totally seeing things through my distorted lens. The lens where all anger had been pushed down, unprocessed. I was told anger was not good. I was assuming what I learned as a child was true. Anger was bad. So, I had to have ways to support my learned beliefs rather than seeking the truth, figuring out the real truth about righteous and unrighteous anger.

It is amazing how many things man has discovered in science that agree with what the Bible says. I wonder if the scientist muses to God, "You actually were telling the truth," to which God replies, "I do that quite a lot, people are always surprised." Jack said a similar thing in POTC1.

I think the answers are there to help us. God wants us to share in all the wonderful things in this world, all the great things we have created. He doesn't enjoy seeing people suffer. He doesn't kill them because they won't do what He wants. He can't. He gave us free will. He suffers right along with us. He cries. He is angry when people misuse their power to hurt other people. It is we who can't see because our lenses aren't clear. We don't see as God sees. The only way we are even going to come close is not by fixing our neighbor, but by fixing ourselves with the help of God and our friends.

God uses people to get his work done. Once our own grids are cleared and are being dealt with, we can be about the business of being all we were meant to be, living life to its fullest.

So, are you living life to the fullest, being all you were meant to be? This is a question we really can't answer for ourselves. Why? Because we look through our own lens to get to the answer. We need to listen to God as He speaks to us through the Holy Spirit, the Bible, circumstances, and the safe people with whom we process life.

God pursues us until the day we die because he loves us. He wants a loving relationship with us like he intended with Adam, to share all the wonderful, glorious, good things he has created for us. However, he gave us free will and will never force anything on us. He just gives us opportunities to accept all the good He has to offer. We always have the final choice.

Remember the legalistic church I talked about in the last chapter? This was one of those many opportunities for me. When my husband decided to get out of the military after 10 ½ years of active-duty service, we moved from Texas to Michigan. While we waited six weeks for our house to close we stayed in a hotel close by to the school our children would be attending. One night at dinner a couple approached us. They were very friendly, asking us if we were new to the area. They told us they were very impressed with how well the children behaved! They then commented that they came there quite often for dinner and had noticed that we said a prayer every time before a meal. They asked us if we had found a church in the area. Since we had not, they invited us to theirs. We ended up going and decided to make it our church for many years.

(A side note here: a lesson we didn't learn until many years later. One picks a church based on a congregation and/or pastors seeing life through a lens very similar to their own. If you grew up in an emotionally dysfunctional family, you would pick an emotionally dysfunctional church. They will be dysfunctional in the same ways you are.)

One of the things this church wanted us to do was to get baptized even though both my husband and I, being raised as a Roman Catholic, had been baptized as infants. They wanted us to tell our story to the congregation aloud and then recite a Bible verse that had a special meaning to us. Talk about uncomfortable. You bet! Talk about opportunity and choice. You bet! Something deep inside was whispering, go on, "do it." So, I did.

I had no idea what verse to pick. All I could pray was, "God, I have no idea what to pick, *help me find a verse!*" I was agitated and afraid but not angry! I was reading Psalm 139 in a devotional and came upon verses 23–24. I thought to myself (or was it that whisper again), "This works. How about this one?" So I picked it.

"Search me, O God, and know my heart: try me, and know my thoughts: And see if there be any wicked way in me and lead me to the way everlasting."

(Psalms 139:23–24, New King James Version [NKJV])

Personally, I now prefer *The Message*. I don't see myself as a "wicked" person.

Investigate my life, Oh God, find out everything about me; cross examine and test me, get a clear picture of what I'm about; see for yourself whether I've done anything wrong - then guide me on the road to eternal life.

(Psalms 139:23–24, *The Message*)

I didn't know the things I was doing were dysfunctional or wrong. It was what I had been taught as a child. I very much like Dr. Henry Cloud and Dr. John Townsend's book, *It's Not My Fault*. In it they have a great quote which I use quite often: "It's not your fault, but it is your problem!" I think that's pretty much how God looks at our grid. All blame does is slow us down and put us on a backward spiral.

I now know that it was another whisper from God. God has continued to use this verse every day. He changes me in some way and brings opportunity into my life every day. So let me ask you one more time if I can. Are you living life to the fullest, being all God intended you to be?

CHAPTER SEVEN:
WITHIN OUR POWER

"The Only Rules That Really Matter Are These: What a Man Can Do and What a Man Can't Do" (POTC1)
What rules has Jesus left for us?

My favorite conversation in all the movies is the one between Captain Sparrow and Will in POTC1. Will needs to rescue his damsel in distress, Elizabeth, and the only one who will help him is Jack. They have commandeered a ship from the Royal Navy, escaped the port, and are out in open water. Will is telling Jack that his father had left his mother and him when he was a tiny lad to go to sea. They never saw his father again.

When Will's mother died, Will, then 10 years old, left England to find his father. In a previous conversation, Jack made a comment which led Will to believe that Jack knew Will's father. Now that they are out of danger and have plenty of time on the open waters, Will confronts Jack and says, "You knew my father!" Once Jack realizes that this question can't be avoided and Will will continue to ask until he gets an answer, he tells Will that he did, in fact, know Will's father and knew him quite well. Jack then adds that Will's father was a *good* man and a *good* pirate. Upon hearing the word pirate, Will becomes insulted, and he draws his cutlass in defense of his father. Jack is at the helm and has his back to Will, but hearing the cutlass being drawn, he says in a caring, empathetic, and fatherly voice, "Put it away son, it's not worth you getting beat again." (Jack is referencing their earlier sword fight in the blacksmith shop.) Will, sounding like a rebellious teenager, says "*You* didn't beat me! You ignored the rules of engagement. In a fair fight, I would have killed you." Jack turns and looks at Will and replies, "Then that's not much incentive for me to fight fair, then, is it?" Jack turns back to the wheel and releases the boom which swings in Will's direction. After hanging Will out over the side of the ship via the boom, Jack says with a loving and firm voice as a father would do, "The only rules that really matter are these, What a man can do and what a man can't do!" Jack gives a few examples to ensure Will understands before returning him to the ship.

That's a good description of Christianity. We can choose to follow Jesus or not. But we were created by God for relationship. The only way we are going to reconcile our relationship with God is to accept what God said about Jesus' sacrifice as the only payment He will accept. And it has already been paid!! So, we can relax and get about God's plan to make this world as close to heaven as we possibly can. You need to realize that we can never do it by ourselves because we are not perfect. Our human nature wants to add all these rules and guidelines to determine if you are a Christian. Even Jesus summed it up into two rules or laws.

> "Just then a religion scholar stood up with a question to test Jesus. 'Teacher, what do I need to do to get eternal life?' He answered, 'What's written in God's Law? How do you interpret it?'
>
> He said, 'That you love the Lord your God with all your passion and prayer and muscle and intelligence—and that you love your neighbor as well as you do yourself.'
>
> 'Good answer!' said Jesus. 'Do it and you'll live.'"
>
> (Luke 10:25–28, *The Message*)

So, it really doesn't matter if others think we are Christians. The only rules that matter are the two Jesus gives us. In other words, the conviction of our own heart that we love God and love our neighbor.

So much damage is done to Christians and non-believers with all these extra rules and laws. Too many dos and don'ts. In reality, as we walk our *own* journey, we will be convicted by the Holy Spirit in His own perfect time. The Holy Spirit will tell us what Jesus wants us to alter in our lives in order to love God and our neighbor the way He intends. It was not designed for man to do so.

Each of us is unique; each of us has a different journey. Jack's father, Captain Teague, tells Jack, "It's not about living forever, Jackie, it's about living with yourself forever." We want to define and label everyone Christian or non-Christian. Christians may live forever, but that is only the beginning. We have to transform to become like Jesus so we can live with ourselves forever. This entails carrying out the original plan God perfectly designed for each of us in His eternal plan before the fall. So, while on earth we are in the process of transforming ourselves and assisting others to bring the Kingdom here, now, just as Jesus did.

CHAPTER EIGHT:
FAN BASE

"All you need to know is that I was rooting for you, mate.
Know that!" (POTC1)
Who's rooting for you?

Jack really was rooting for James Norrington. Jack could see a real possibility for James. James was trapped by society. Jack wanted James to break through to become the man Jack could see, and knew James could be. Although it is only hinted at in the movie, there was a history between Jack and James. Jack had known James when James was six and Jack was 16. Jack knew the type of family that shaped James. He knew that James was capable of much more and could enjoy freedom if he let go of his past.

Isn't this what God wants for us? God is *always* rooting for us. He knows the great possibilities that await us. He knows who He intended us to be. God uses people to guide us on that path. Just like He used Jack and James to help each other at various times. Although they seemed at odds most of the time, they were safe people rooting for each other!

Many of us are a lot like James. We have been shaped by our past. We seek out a community that supports our past. We believe it is the only right way we should live. It may be all we know and are comfortable with.

Most of us do not like change. We are afraid that becoming different will make us unacceptable to our present community. We are afraid we won't fit. But the underlying fear is the *fear of being alone*. This is a very normal and accepted reason.

We were created for relationship. Before we can even try to explore who we are and what we were created to be, we have to have people rooting for us! Many of us don't know how to begin picking the people we want rooting for us. Usually, we rely on what we were taught, what we observed as a child. Doctors John Townsend and Henry Cloud have written a book entitled *Safe People*, which I would highly recommend you read before you pick the people rooting for you!

In the book, they describe what safe and unsafe people look like. Does this mean unsafe people are bad? Absolutely not, but they may not be rooting for us. It also does not mean that all our friends and acquaintances are safe. Out of the 12 apostles, Jesus picked three to be intimate friends: Peter, James, and John. According to Drs. Cloud and Townsend, safe people are on your side, they want what's best for you (even though it may be painful for one or both of you at times), and they want you to be all God created you to be.

Jesus was the ultimate safe friend. He modeled how a safe person looks and acts. He called Peter to task several times for not wanting what God wanted for Jesus. Here he was teaching Peter to be a safe person. Jesus confronts Peter with love. He tells Peter, "You are a stumbling block to me, you do not have in mind the things of God, but the things of men", (Matthew 16:23, NIV1984). That was not a pleasant scene for Peter, but Jesus told him the truth. It may have been hard for Peter to hear but it was making him all God needed him to be in the future.

There are no perfectly safe people. You want people who are aware of what safe people are and are growing to be safe. You will work together in helping each other be safe and you will be safe for other people.

In God's plan our parents were supposed to be the safe people bringing us up in the ways of the Lord (e.g., being safe for others). Unfortunately, after the fall, things fell apart. So please don't assume your family is safe just because they are family. And *please* remember just because they are not safe to confide in does not mean they are not good people. They can still love you very much. They, too, someday, may become safe. Some of you are very fortunate in that you have a family or parents who are safe people. Some of you have the great misfortune of growing up in a very unsafe home. *The important thing is that you learn who is safe, who is not, and never assume.* If you have five to six people in your lifetime who are safe for you, you are very fortunate. I have four.

Your small group should be safe just like Jesus' group of 12 was safe. This doesn't mean all of your safe group are close to you but, in general, they are safe. Remember, Jesus picked Peter, James, and John out of the 12 to be His intimate friends. All of the apostles were great apostles and safe. Judas of Iscariot had to fulfill the prophecy. He was the one to betray Jesus and hand him over to the Jewish leaders. He became possessed by Satan. After that he was unsafe and Satan had all the control.

"Above all else, guard your heart because for it is the wellspring of life.", (Proverbs 4:23, NIV1984)

Notice "above all else." That means before you do anything else (e.g., witness, ministry, working, etc.) guard your heart, which I believe means find your safe people. Once you have your safe person or people (and we should always be striving to get more), you are ready for the world. It needs to be more than your spouse if you are married. In the beginning, God started off with three safe persons (Father, Son, Holy Spirit).

After many years of therapy my husband and I learned to deal with and process our feelings with each other. Our children began to learn to do the same but that was about as far as it got. Then through a set of circumstances we were moved to California leaving our adult children behind. This began our next level of transformation. We have discussed in an earlier chapter how God can use circumstances to lead us. I had gotten a job at a church to become an assistant to one of the pastors. One of my assignments was to head up the Stephen Ministry program by becoming a Stephen leader. They were going to send me to that training to learn the basics for Stephen ministry. As far as leadership went, I didn't have a clue. My husband and I had recently heard about this leadership course called "Ultimate Leadership," which came highly recommended. We talked it over and decided it would be just the thing I needed. I had never been in a leadership position (other than as a mother) and I felt this could give me the confidence I needed. Little did I know at the time this was another step up in my transformation!

This course is where I learned about safe people. A safe person is

1. someone who is for you (grace).

2. someone who wants you to be all God intended for you to be (truth).

3. someone who is going to be there for you when you need them (time).

They offer grace just as God does and gives forgiveness. They understand when we do mess up. They love us all the same, that unconditional love we all need. That is not to say there are not consequences for our actions. That's where the second quality comes in, truth. Criticism can be good if it helps us change for the better. In my family of origin the only time I heard from my parents or siblings as a child was to tell me I was doing something wrong. Needless to say, I carried that with me and was defensive in my adult life. This was because when I did something wrong love was withheld until it was fixed. Love was always conditional. When I discovered this, in order to be able to take criticism from my husband, he would first have to remind me, "Marty, I'm on your side and I love you very much. I need to tell you something that I think will help you." That may sound silly, but I needed to be reminded of that unconditional love until it became embedded in my brain. Fortunately, it didn't take as long to accept the other message once I had been convinced of his unconditional love.

Often, we don't like to hear what safe people have to say, or perhaps we are expecting a certain reaction when we say something. From all my prior experiences, I sought some professional help when I was working through a lot of this. I was familiar with the therapist, and I knew he was a safe person. He told you straight out what the truth was, and even though it didn't feel good at times I knew he had my best interest at heart. Several weeks into my visits with him I was sharing that during a particularly hard grieving experience I called a family member to share my grief and get some comfort and understanding. Instead, they had complete disregard for my grief. All they could talk about was their own similar experiences and how they got over it. They thought this would help me through my grief when what I needed was someone to listen.

I was hurt and angry and wanted some empathy from the counselor. What I got was the truth and an example which has helped me and others many, many times! He looked across the room at me and noticed I was drinking a diet Coke (my drink of choice at the time). He said to me in an inquisitive voice, "You really like diet Coke, don't you?" I nodded and he said in a louder frustrated voice, "Then *why* do you keep putting your quarters in a 7 Up machine trying to get diet Coke? 7 Up is a great, refreshing drink when you want 7 Up, but *not* when you want diet Coke!"

I am a very visual person, and that image said it all for me. But not when it was delivered. At first, I was angry. I wanted empathy and he wanted to talk about diet Coke. Wouldn't anyone listen to my hurt? Or was it unjustified and I should let it go?

Did I get the sympathy I wanted from him? NO! But I didn't need sympathy, I needed truth. Thankfully, he was listening, he did care, and he did help. He cared enough for me that he was willing to tell the truth and risk what I thought of him. All for my best interest no matter how I responded. By the way, later in the session he let me know he was a diet Coke machine! That experience was so powerful that I have a picture of a 7 Up and diet Coke machine in my office.

So, I ask you, are you a safe person and who do you have rooting for you, mate?

CHAPTER NINE: PRESENCE

A Compass that Doesn't Point North
What is it that Jesus wants most?

Captain Jack Sparrow's compass didn't point north. In fact, many thought his compass was broken. He told Elizabeth, "My compass is *unique*." (POTC1) This is true. Jack's compass pointed to the thing the person holding the compass wanted the most.

We all have a compass like Jack, and we use it to guide us through life. Many of us set our course, then plow down anything and anyone that gets in our way. We tend to live in the future where we think our destination lies. When we are not focusing on our destination we tend to live in the past, trying to figure out what is holding us back.

What Jack understood was that the journey is the destination. It's the getting where we are going that life is all about. It is what is happening right now as I type this page and you are reading it. It is living in this present moment.

This doesn't mean that we don't have goals. Jesus had goals. He came to restore the relationship between each of us with the Father and was willing to do whatever it took to make it happen. He didn't decide how He was going to do this. He left those details up to the Father. He stayed focused on the here and now and how the present would help restore the relationship.

Sometimes, we are so caught up in how we are going to achieve our own goals that we lose sight of God's goal. Again, we look to the future, and we don't see what is going on NOW.

For argument's sake let us assume Jesus has a compass like Jack's. It doesn't point north, but it points to the thing that He wants the most, that would be the relationship He wants with you and me. He will use the people around us and with us to make it happen, if we let Him lead, just as He uses us to draw others closer to Him.

We all have times like this when we don't know what we want. We tell ourselves we want one thing, but we are miserable and confused, not enjoying what it is we think we want. In fact, we really have no idea what we want. Still, we fight the compass and try to get it to point to where we think we want to go. We'd be much better off if we learned to go where the compass leads. That's where transformation takes place.

Transformation is a process where we go from being the person we are to the person God intended for us to be when He created us. He has had a glorious plan for us all along.

I know what I'm doing. I have it all planned out—plans to take care of you, not abandon you, plans to give you the future you hope for.

(Jeremiah 29:11, *The Message*)

It boils down to trust. Can we trust Jesus' compass? Can we trust that the Father's plan is a good plan for us, that He really wants us to have a great future? We need to get out of our comfort zone and take a risk.

I really don't recall in any of the movies when Captain Sparrow was in his comfort zone. Perhaps when he was at the helm, but even then, he wasn't in charge. He was just keeping the ship afloat, the people aboard safe! Jack seemed to me to be constantly squirming and uncomfortable. He was always in a jam. However, he just went with the flow, he always seemed to have a positive, happy-go-lucky attitude. He knew he had a compass that would always lead him to what he wanted most even if he didn't know what that really was. He dealt with things head on.

Never was Jack's first choice to be in a ticklish situation. Nonetheless, when that's where he was, he turned toward it and embraced it. Take for example the kraken scene. Jack was going to be pulled down with his ship the *Black Pearl* into Davy Jones's locker (POTC2). There, he would abide with his greatest fear for eternity. Turns out for Captain Sparrow his greatest fear was himself. We talked about that in Chapter Five. My point is that Jack knew immediately that he couldn't run, and he turned toward the kraken, confronting it head on, sword in hand.

Jesus called everyone who wanted to follow Him to get out of their comfort zone. Leave your job, leave your family, leave your religious practices, give up your money, give up your possessions. It is not wrong to have any of those things. He gives them to us, but He wanted people around Him who were willing to take a risk, to get out of their comfort zone, grow, and transform. He wanted them to follow a compass that didn't point North.

When I was young, I used to think I had to do all of the giving up all at once. As I look back, I realize that at one time or another all of those things had been on the line. I can say that at one time or another we did end up losing a job or possession. We disagreed with a denomination, leaving the church, changed the behavior patterns of our alcoholic families, and lost our possessions in a fire. God had something much better in mind in every situation. Something I had never even dreamed. So, before you get scared, realize it doesn't happen all at once. It takes a lifetime. I specifically remember when I first read about giving up my family. If you remember, I'm the adult child of an alcoholic. That means I had black and white thinking. So, to me, that could only mean one thing. Abandon my family (possibly never see them again) and become a missionary. That didn't sound too loving to me especially since I had a husband, a baby girl 14 months old, and one on the way, not to mention all the rest of my family. Fortunately, I was so sick with morning sickness at the time and my husband had just started his commission in the U.S. Army, that I decided to put these verses on hold to deal with at a later time. I don't think I was reading my compass correctly. Once again, the Holy Spirit was there to help me in this circumstance. For me I needed to relax and hone my listening skills to learn how to read this compass that doesn't point north.

CHAPTER TEN: DISPENSING GRACE

"But Why Is the Rum Always Gone?" (POTC1)
Or is it grace that is missing?

Jack and Elizabeth are marooned on a deserted island. Jack apparently has been marooned on this island before. Aside from watching his ship being sailed away by Barbosa for the second time, Jack doesn't seem too worried. You see, Jack is a survivor, and he knows exactly what is needed to stay alive. Because he has been here before, he knows that this island has what is needed.

It is always important to understand the time in history and the culture when trying to understand what is being said. But many times, we just take words and apply them to what we know and experience and assume we have the answer. Jack knew there was rum on the island. Rum was used on the ship to add to water to kill the germs. In that time in history, water was not safe to drink.

The first time we hear Jack use the phrase "But why is the Rum always gone?" was when he and Elizabeth were marooned on an island. The first night on the island, Jack drank too much rum, went to sleep, and didn't awaken until morning. When he opened his eyes, he saw Elizabeth burning all the shade trees, the rum, and supplies. He jumped up, in a panic when he realized what Elizabeth was doing. He was most upset that she was burning the rum.

Elizabeth insisted that the fire would attract the British ships searching for her and that they would come and rescue them. Again, Jack asked why the rum was gone. Elizabeth insisted, "Rum is a vile drink and turns even the most respectable men into scoundrels." Jack left in a rage, separating himself to keep from harming Elizabeth. As a side note, this was a very good example of what we can do when we become angry. In Jack's case it was a righteous anger because if the British don't come, she had destroyed their chance for survival. I also believe that Elizabeth was displaying some passive aggressive behavior instead of talking to Jack about drinking too much rum. However, that could be a discussion for a whole other book.

As it turned out, Elizabeth was right. British sailors spotted the smoke and rescued them. But let's say there were no search parties, the fire burned out, and they were still stranded on the island. They wouldn't have survived very long. Man can go a pretty long time without food but not so without drink. Rum was used to purify the water. It is most likely that a good portion of that rum was mixed with water, and they could have held out for perhaps a month or maybe longer.

In our zealousness to make sure that the new Christian understands all the laws or ways of Jesus we often forget the grace. We even view grace as Elizabeth viewed rum. Jesus told us very clearly that he came to fulfill the law, that now all things fall under just two laws: remember the code. This takes an enormous amount of grace. I really don't think the world could survive without God's grace. It began in the garden, and He has been giving it to us ever since. Likewise, we should be showing grace to others. In Christianity, Grace is unmerited favor. Many times, we are afraid of giving people too much grace. Can there ever be too much grace?

The key word here is *afraid*.

"There is no fear in love. But perfect love drives out fear, because fear has to do with punishment. The one who fears is not made perfect in love.",

(1 John 4:18, NIV1984)

We really have to trust God. We are not responsible for others' actions. God can see into the heart, but we can't. This is about a relationship with Jesus. This is about their relationship with Jesus and about our relationship with Jesus. The more we get to know Him the more we understand Him and the more we want to become all He wants us to be. So, only by knowing someone over time and having a relationship with them could you possibly share that relationship with them.

There is no grace when we decide someone is not a Christian based on a movie they went to see, a group they were hanging out with, whether or not they go to church, if they are gay, or by some sin in their life. We were never created to judge. As I recall that job was given to Jesus. So, let's encourage each other to grow our relationships together and with Jesus by spreading the grace. There is plenty to go around.

CHAPTER ELEVEN: GRACE AND TRUST

"Of the two of us, I am the only one who hasn't committed mutiny. Therefore, my word is the one we'll be trusting." (POTC2)
Grace is free; trust is earned.

Jesus says the same to us. "Of the two of us I am the only one who hasn't sinned. Therefore, *my* word is the one we'll be trusting. On the other hand, *my* love is free and available to all who wish to receive it." So, when we take His love freely, why is it we still seem reluctant to trust Him? Unfortunately, our human nature often prevents us from automatically trusting someone just because they say we can. Trust is earned (or lost or withheld) through experience. It can't be forced. Jesus is willing to take all the time and experience we need with Him to earn that Trust, but we have to initiate the process. Remember, He won't make us. This is why just a prayer time, scripture reading, devotional, or Sunday going to church day won't work.

What is needed here is, "Okay, Jesus, I don't trust you. I want to trust you, but you will have to earn that trust. Please show me ways where I can trust you or that You have already been there for me. Help me to be aware of your presence."

Then you need to start looking around. Remember, God uses people, situations, circumstances, prayers, the Bible, and other ways to communicate with you. Look for the miracles. Many people believe if they pray for something and don't get what they want, then that means they can't trust God. He doesn't answer the prayer the way they want. (On a side note, God is not a Disneyland *abba*. This is what I am talking about.) God always does what is best for us even when we don't agree with it. Let me give you an example from my life.

Back in the late '70s, early '80s, my husband was in the Army, and we were stationed in Europe. My mother came to visit us at Christmas. We had two little girls, ages six and four, and a five-month-old son whom she hadn't met. When she got off the plane, she had a lump on her neck the size of a grapefruit. When she saw the look on my face she said, "Don't worry I'm going to get it checked when I get back." I was horrified. She basically had been afraid it was cancer, that if she had seen a doctor who confirmed her suspicions, he might not have let her come to meet her grandson. She knew my husband had a three-year tour of duty. She was afraid she might never get to see him.

We managed to get a doctor to see her there. We also made her promise she would see one as soon as she returned. When she did, tests confirmed that the growth was cancerous. The Red Cross sent for me to come home.

My mother had only Social Security as an income and was unable to care for herself. My husband put in for a compassionate reassignment and we took my mother on as a dependent. While waiting for my husband to return to the states, I took Mom to radiation every day. The growth responded very well and shrank considerably. Unfortunately, since she had waited so long to see a doctor, surgery was not an option.

My husband's reassignment was to Fort Hood, Texas. Mom would receive her treatments just a few hours from our home. At the time, Brooke Army Medical Center in San Antonio was one of the best hospitals in the United States for cancer treatment. The doctors were encouraged. They thought that with the chemotherapy, Mom could last a year, and maybe two or three. Who could say at that point? We found the perfect house in Gainesville, 10 minutes from Fort Hood. It even had a little house out back with a small kitchen and bath. We couldn't believe how God provided. We made our offer and called my mom. She was so happy. Two days later, the owner changed her mind and didn't want to sell the house. We were devastated.

It was perfect. How could God lead us there and then we don't get it? We ended up with a four-bedroom home. It turned out to be much better for our budget. Two weeks after my mom got to our house, she had a bad reaction to the chemotherapy. That was August. We tried alternatives, then in October I told Mom I thought quality of life was much better than quantity. Tears of joy filled her face.

From October through January, we talked and bonded like we never had. She had been an alcoholic most of her life. She stopped drinking when I was nine, but she was never there for us emotionally. Whenever I wanted a hug, she always said she wasn't affectionate.

My dad died when I was 19. Now I was 31 and my mom became the mom I never had. She gave my children so many wonderful memories. One daughter was in kindergarten and was learning to write her numbers. She always made her fives backwards. My mom made me go to the bank and get her several rolls of quarters. When my daughter brought her paper home and would jump up on the bed to show her Grammy, she would get a quarter for every correct 5. To this day. my daughter can't write a five without thinking of her Grammy.

My other daughter remembers that all the walls in her Grammy's room were covered with the papers the girls colored for her. Floor to ceiling.

Mom's goal was to make it to Christmas. She did. Christmas afternoon she had a small transient ischemic attack stroke. She was bedridden from that time forward.

One day we were talking in her room about how much she loved to watch the snow come down. How pretty it was. I told her I wished I could help her out, but in Texas there wasn't much chance. Several hours later I was throwing back the curtains and pushing her bed to the window. It was unbelievable how hard it was snowing. Both of us were holding hands and crying.

She used to tell me she'd always wondered why God gave me to her. In fact, she was not so happy about it at the time. She'd had plans and I messed them up. I was a late-in-life baby. When I was born, my brother was 22, my sisters 16 and 14. But now she put her arms around me, pulled me close like a mother would a child, and said, "Now I know why God gave you to me."

All these years…she started to weep, and through her tears she rocked back and forth saying, "I love you so much!" Then when she stopped crying, she started singing, "You are my sunshine, my only sunshine…" As I sat up, I noticed the snow was gone and sunshine was streaming through the windows!

Did God know what was best? Yes! And because He has done things over and over like that in my life, I would have to say *yes*, I can trust Him. Take a look back in your life. Are there incidents in your life where God stepped in? If not, then watch the future because, believe me, if you have asked God to earn your trust, He will. He is very patient and as I said before He is always there loving you with His never-ending unconditional love. He will pursue you all the days of your life, but in the end the choice is yours.

When you look back, write these memories down in a safe place. As you think of more, add to your list. My next book is going to be about the very subject of how God is constantly performing miracles in our life, but we are not trained to see them. Many times, we just call it fate or coincidence.

CHAPTER TWELVE: DISCERNMENT

Governor Swann: "He's a pirate!"
Will: "And a GOOD man." (POTC3)
So who is he really?

Labels are dangerous, yet we use them all the time. We humans have this great need to put people in little boxes, usually marked with the first label that comes to mind. The tragedy is that, once we label a person, we don't bother to explore that person any further. We already assume we "know" what this person is all about! Our parents did it, their parents did it, all the way back to Adam and Eve. If we're honest with ourselves, we do it, too.

As discussed in previous chapters, we were created for relationship and never created to judge. That is God's job. But Adam and Eve changed all that by eating of the tree of knowledge of good and evil.

Let's first take a look at the movie and identify all the labels that we infer or place on the characters. These labels could come from the labels characters gave each other, labels others gave them, or labels we gave them:

1. Governor Swann: *doting father* (his own label), *not so bright* (hinted at by Norrington).

2. Elizabeth: *a woman, rebellious, naive, needs saving, needs to be cared for, pampered, weak teenager, fragile, immature, a leader, thinks on her feet, rises to the occasion, ill tempered.*

3. Will: *stick-in-the-mud, indecisive, told what to think, no mind of his own, afraid but needing to hide it, stubborn, immature, feels abandoned, loving, wants to be loved.*

4. Norrington: *pompous, arrogant, bitter, conceited, prim and proper, "British," sees only his own way, a need for acceptance.*

5. Jack: *a drunk, crazy, homosexual, self-absorbed, cares about no one but Jack, conniving, uneducated, pirate, good man.*

6. Barbosa: *evil or bad guy, cruel, hateful, likes to watch people squirm, selfish, will let no one get in his way even if it means death.*

7. Pintel and Ragetti: *cruel, stupid, homosexual partners, no common sense, wonder how they made it this far.*

8. Cotton: *dumb old fumbling man not worth much.*

9: Gibbs: *drunk, coward, little sea knowledge, mostly myths, no sense of responsibility, can't be depended on.*

10: Anna Maria: *witch and other rhyming words, educated, skilled.*

Granted, this is what the movie implies about each character and wants you to think about them. If you think about it, you probably accepted those suggestions without another thought. Perhaps, like we do in real life.

After the third movie, our views are changed somewhat. Certainly, mine were! And, after reading all the books about the characters' youth and how they met, all my views of each character drastically changed.

The point is that the more you get to know about someone, the more you see them as a whole person. If you notice, in the movies Jack seems to be the one to find the good in all these people even when we can't. In fact, none of the accusations made were completely true. All of them were based on people you or other characters knew. Perhaps it's worth going back to rethink your views of them.

Now let's take a look at Jesus' ministry. Over and over, He was accused of hanging out with *thieves, robbers, scum of the earth* (Matthew

9:10–12; Mark 2:15–17; Luke 5:29–31, 19:5–7, NIV1984). He was labeled *rebel, troublemaker, rabble-rouser, blasphemer, Satan,* etc.

Our take on Jesus is much different, but we have the luxury of knowing the end of His story. What if that had not happened for us? Many of us just listen to what others tell us and never really find out for ourselves. If you are a Christian, and you never had the opportunity to find out about Jesus from family, friends, or church, would you really take the time to find out for yourself? What do you know about Jesus that someone hasn't told you? If we don't personally explore our faith, we really can't claim to be Christians!

Jesus has a dream for you. He can see what and who you are. *Not* what you are to others, but what He created you to be. In fact, that is all He ever sees. Until you see this vision for yourself, you cannot begin to work with Jesus to grow the Kingdom! This will be an ongoing, lifetime process.

The same process goes on with people we meet. Do we accept what others or society have told us about this person or do we find out for ourselves and come to our own conclusions? Are you really aware of your thought processes? If you wrote down every thought you had during one day you would fill a rather large book. Some thoughts come so fast we are not even aware of them. Let me challenge you to keep a list of thoughts for one week. You don't have to do it for the whole day. Pick five minutes or so and track your thoughts. As a suggestion, do it when you arrive home and re-engage with your family for the day. Other good times would be when you meet with people for lunch or after work for happy hour. Remember, we are not judging any thoughts. No thought going into your notebook is right or wrong. We are just identifying them. At first, it will be extremely hard, but stick with it. You are training your mind to be aware of your thoughts. Your thoughts can be all over the map and they don't have to make sense. We just want to track them. If you've completed this challenge, were you surprised by your thoughts?

Let's compare the thought processes of Will and Governor Swann about Jack. Governor Swann's go something like this: He's a pirate. Pirates are thieves, liars, bad and evil. Therefore, Jack is a thief, liar, bad, and evil! Will, on the other hand, analyzes it differently. "Jack is a pirate. Pirates I have heard about are evil thieves and liars. Jack saved Elizabeth's life; Jack helped me find Elizabeth and save her. Therefore, Jack is a pirate and a good man." Will uses only what he learned from his encounters with Jack, not what others say about him.

Governor Swann has that same opportunity. Jack has just saved his daughter from drowning, then saved her again from the other pirates. Governor Swann decides to stick with the label.

We mostly judge based on the experience of others. Until you have lived in community with a person, you really know nothing about them. Jesus lived in community with the disciples. They shared their souls deeply with one another, for three years, seven days a week, 24 hours a day. This level of sharing happens over time; you just don't sit down one day and do it.

The next time you catch yourself making a statement about someone or labeling them, ask yourself if you have enough evidence for this to hold up in a court of law.

The example I like to use is when churchgoers are talking with each other and are interested in a person. One of the first questions asked is, "Is he/she Christian?" I think the better questions would be, "Who is this person that God has created? And how can I walk alongside and be a safe person for them?" Isn't that what Christ did when he was here on earth? I would like to stress here that this would not be a co-dependent relationship! You must first know yourself, your strengths and weaknesses, and have some very healthy boundaries in place. Jack knew what he could and couldn't do and what was up for discussion (choice).

Some food for thought that may help you understand some more about the process of living in community is to watch the series "Chosen".

It is a free app you can download on your phone, laptop, or streaming devices (Apple App Store, Google Play, Roku, Apple TV, and Amazon Fire). It is starting its fourth season. It is free to anyone all over the world. It is about Jesus and how he lived in community with the disciples. It is told through the eyes of disciples based on the book of Matthew. This is the most powerful and real interpretation I have ever seen. I highly recommend it whether you are a believer or not. There is no hidden agenda here. Just real people living real life.

CHAPTER THIRTEEN: UNPACKING A SEALED HEART

"Man, if you lock your heart away, you'll lose it for sure."
(POTC3) Are you a superficial Christian or authentic?

What was Jack referring to when he told Will he would lose his heart for sure? Can one really lock one's heart away? In most cases we don't "choose" to lock our heart away. Remember that grid we talked about in Chapter Five? If you are unaware of what your true feelings are and how to correctly process them, then you can't possibly really know what's on your heart or even where it is! "Above all else, guard your heart, for it is the wellspring of life" (Psalms 4:23, NIV1984).

If you don't know where it is, how are you going to guard it? I remember when I first got introduced to all this "Christian speak" or "Christianese" as some call it. People were running around saying, "Oh, I have Jesus in my heart!" with a big smile on their face. And here I was thinking inside, "Well, maybe you should let him out so we can all see what He looks like!" I believe that is one of the best ways we can "witness" (another Christianese word) to people about Jesus is by telling people our own life story and how we are changing through Jesus. Because when the "rubber meets the road" as they say, these are the only facts that they can't refute. Then the choice is theirs!

So back to what Jack was observing in Will. Will had tunnel vision. He decided to see only one thing. He would rescue his father from Davy Jones's ship, even though he might die doing so, might lose the love of his life, and would betray his only friend, Jack. That was his plan.

Will was not allowing himself to look inside and invest time to learn who he really was. He made a promise to his biological father, a man he had just met. The promise was irrational when he made it and it came from anger (passive aggressive). Will was angry that his father had abandoned him and his mother to go to sea when Will was a baby. Now, because of his stubbornness, and to prove he was a better man than his father by not abandoning him, he was going to see his plan through.

Jack was speaking from experience about heart loss. For many years he had tried to lock away parts of his heart, unaware he was doing it. His past included many experiences and hurts he would rather forget and put away.

This approach has its problems. One is that it doesn't work. We keep pushing memories and hurts down until one day we can't hold anymore. Then they start coming out in different ways, blurring our vision like we talked about in Chapter Five. Fortunately for Jack, he was forced to deal with it all when he was sent down to Davy Jones's Locker. There is a scene where multiple images of Jack are running around on the *Pearl*. Each Jack character represents a different personality. Each is only capable of having one feeling. Jack is very comfortable with some of these parts of himself; others he fears. They may have been aspects of himself he had buried deeply to survive while growing up. Consequently, he had never developed these parts of himself.

The angry Jack gets to see his angry self, angry at Elizabeth for getting him here, and angry at himself for falling for her scam. This angry self now has to deal with all the other parts. The happy Jack, the lackadaisical Jack, the irresponsible Jack, the people pleaser (the one he kills), and the child Jack. I have to admit that when Jack leaves Davy Jones's Locker he does seem more integrated and able to make good decisions. Jack can now understand what happens when you lock your feelings away within your heart.

Locking your heart away these days is pretty common. Think about the song by Simon and Garfunkel, "I Am a Rock" (written by Paul Simon; lyrics© Universal Music Publishing Group):

A winter's day

In a deep and dark December

I am alone

Gazing from my window to the streets below

On a freshly fallen silent shroud of snow

I am a rock

• • •

And a rock feels no pain

And an island never cries

(For complete lyrics see:

https://www.lyrics.com/lyric/15269428/Paul+Simon/I+Am+a+Rock

In the song the singer is so hurt he just doesn't want to deal with feelings anymore. So, he/she makes a decision to lock his heart (feelings) away and never deal with them. Most of us don't even know what is in our hearts. Then, to top it off, we become Christians and invite Jesus into our hearts. It is a nice metaphor, but what does it really mean? Think about it. When we look in the mirror, do we really know who is looking back? Have we really taken any time to get to know ourselves? In the 1900s, one certainly did not talk about these things. If you did, it was mostly behind closed doors. If you did display them in public, you were thought of as being mentally ill. Especially women. There was a rancid stigma attached to anyone believed to have mental illness. In fact, people would step away from you as though your illness was contagious. The avoidance was more likely fear that you would bring up a feeling or event they may have experienced and were afraid to share with anyone else.

Sure, we all share things with our Starbucks friends, but that's because they will tell us what we *think* we need to hear. We usually only share with these friends the things that we can justify, that we share no responsibility of being at fault in the situation. We want that friend to agree with us and support our view. We usually want to feel better when we leave than when we arrived. We place ourselves basically out of the situation we have described or having no blame in the reason the situation occurred. Basically, this is called triangulation. Remember Adam and Eve. They wanted God to believe what happened was no fault of their own. All the blame was transferred. Fortunately for us and them God saw right through it. He was a real friend because He told them the truth and the consequences. We have to have friends that are safe. The safe friends are the friends we can be totally honest with. We then have an open mind to listen. Some friends are dinner and a movie friends, while others are Starbucks friends to share a cup of coffee with. This is where we need to know the difference between those friends and our safe friends. We need to have boundaries in place. We need to know who is safe for us to share our heart with and they with us.

Remember when I told you in an earlier chapter about having an incident with my husband and taking the problem to the family pastor. I honestly believe now that God was totally protecting me. Because we had recently moved to Michigan I didn't have any friends to go to Starbucks with, to spill my broken heart to. Had it gone that way, I would have been headed for a lawyer and wouldn't be able to say my husband and I have been married for 53+ years, still each other's best friend. Side note: We had to learn to be safe with each other.

So, if parts of your heart are locked away you need to figure out what those parts look like, to find "safe" people to share and grow with.

CHAPTER FOURTEEN: COMMITMENT

"You'll have to do it alone, mate. I see no profit in it for me."
(POTC1)
What is in it for you?

Jack, being considered the scum of the earth and having nothing, knew from the very start what was in it for himself. He knew that Will was a blacksmith and made swords. Therefore, Will was of a lower class. But still, Will had a number of skills and capabilities and he could prove useful. Most likely he didn't have a ship and had no nautical skills. He also found out by his last name that Will was the son of his best friend from childhood Billy Turner and Bill's wife who was also a childhood friend of Jack's.

Jack needed to see how much buy-in he had from Will. He knew Will would need to set him free from jail to lead him to the *Black Pearl*. But once he found the ship, Will would have no chance in getting Elizabeth unless he had help. And so, the bartering begins!

Once they have escaped, Jack checks Will's commitment one last time before they board the ship. If Will isn't "all in" then Jack might as well split and find another way off the island in all the chaos. When Will claims he would die for Elizabeth, Jack agrees to go ahead with his original plan.

Doesn't it seem to be human nature to ask, "What's in it for me?" I mean, there's got to be a catch. There's no free lunch, right? So, Jack gets the *Pearl* and Will rescues Elizabeth. What if the circumstances were different? What if Jack said, "You get me out of here. We go to Tortuga, I find a friend, and He will guarantee Elizabeth's safety." Do you think Will would have been so eager then? Same results are there! I don't think so because there is no reason to even begin to trust! Yet we want to tell people the wonderful things Christianity has to offer and expect them to jump right in! Where is the solid relationship? Where is the trust? I think we want to pass the buck and let the "church" do that work for us.

It is time we wake up and realize *you and I* are the church. Each of us as individuals. The only way people are going to find out what's in it for them is by *experiencing* what's in it for you and what's in it for me. And that takes time. A long time. It is a process. At least 30,576 hours. That's how long Jesus spent with the close disciples. And that's what it took to keep the church going.

Let me not forget to mention what's in it for God. All He has ever wanted from the very moment of creation, that one-on-one relationship that you and I by our own free will desire just as much as He does, a relationship that God sacrificed even His Son to get. Sounds like God's in it, as far as I can tell, 100 percent. So, what's really the risk for us? We have to discover who we truly are and learn how to trust.

CHAPTER FIFTEEN:
LIVING VS. PRACTICING

"You need to find yourself a girl, mate!" (POTC1)
Devotions, Bible reading, prayer life,
Sunday School and church attendance.

It's Will's first encounter with Jack. Rumors fly fast and he has heard everything about this pirate. This pirate who has put his one true love (Elizabeth) in danger. Never mind that the pirate saved her life. Will could prove himself a man and capture the pirate. No holds barred!

Jack and Will are sparring. Jack is looking at all the swords hanging around him. There must be at least a hundred. As they continue to spar Jack asks of Will, "Who makes all these?" Will proudly responds, "I do, and I practice with them at least three hours a day!" Jack's face shows pity and compassion as he says, "You need to get yourself a girl, mate!" Sadly, Will only looks confused.

Unfortunately, as Christians grow, they take on more or longer devotions, increase their prayer life, volunteer at church more, go to more Bible studies, go to church more, read the Bible more, and think, "I am becoming a seasoned or mature Christian or better Christian." Not the case. They are becoming better at their "religion" but forgetting what the purpose for this is. Or as it is said in the Bible, forgetting their first love.

For many people, much of their Christian activity just keeps them from the reality of the *real* world. They are still on a milk diet, still babies. This is for the new Christian. Let me clarify. I am not suggesting stopping these things, but it is time to be out putting to use what God has created us to do, and not stay around a bunch of like-minded people where it is safe. By now, our safety should be the arms of Jesus. "I will never leave you nor forsake you." (Joshua 1:5b, NIV1984). We need to stop proving who we are to the world and start loving the world. By now, our every step should be guided by Jesus.

When we get home, we shouldn't be too tired from work, but too tired from showing Jesus to the world without talking.

I don't do well at memorizing scripture. I can memorize it for the time but ask me a few weeks later to recite it and I'm lucky if I get the gist of it. And citing chapter and verse? Forget that altogether. But it's funny. If I'm out with someone and I need it, the verse comes to me immediately. Mind you, I don't try to recall it, it just comes out.

I think that's what it means when Jesus says, "When they arrest you and hand you over, do not worry beforehand about what you are to say, but say whatever is given you in that hour; for it is not you who speak, but it is the Holy Spirit" (Mark 13:11, NASB95).

Will is practicing, but for what? To be the best swordsman? The reason he should be practicing is to be able to defend himself, to sharpen his mind and to be able to handle whatever comes his way. The only way he can do that is to be out with other swordsmen, sparring with them, not in his shop practicing with himself.

Likewise, we need to be out among the hurting, the sick, and the poor. You don't have to sell your house and become a missionary. Just look at the people and circumstances around you and listen. Actively listen. You will see they are your coworker, your neighbor, the person in front of you in the grocery store. When you show unconditional love and are a safe person, people naturally want to be around you.

Church is a place to get recharged and support, to get back into the broken world and spread the love of Jesus. That's how the acts of the apostles teaches us. Instead, we tell people about Jesus, bring them back to church service on Sunday, or worse yet we send them to church on their own, and then expect the pastor and staff to do the rest. No, we are all in this together and we *all* need to help each other figure out our gifts and talents, to help each other be the best person God intended us to be.

By the end of the movie that is exactly what Jack had done for Will. He helps him mature into a man, make his own decisions, think for himself, not blindly accept what people tell him, rather, research it for himself to find the truth. Does God want us to have any less?

CHAPTER SIXTEEN:
CHECK YOUR VMV

"They done what's right by them.
I can't expect more than that." (POTC1)
What does Jesus expect of you?

The end of the first movie is nearing. Will has saved Elizabeth. Jack has placed that single shot he has been saving into Barbosa, who lays dead. The curse has been lifted and Jack has collected a significant amount of treasure. They are exiting the cave so that Will and Elizabeth can return to Port Royal and Jack to his beloved ship, the *Black Pearl.* Only the crew has taken off without him and now he will be taken back to Port Royal to hang. Is he enraged with the crew? No, he simply says, "They done what's right by them. I can't expect more than that."

So many of us have a vision of a God who sits in heaven just waiting for us to mess up so He can zap us. When all along He has the attitude of, "They just miss the mark, they just don't get it, and they will never be able to fix this problem on their own no matter how hard they try. Having a list of rules to follow doesn't work. I have sent my Son to fix it, to show them by example the way back to Me. Jesus is the only one who understands how to do it. He must be fully human but also maintain his deity. He will fulfill the law, pay the price, and bring the Kingdom. I want my beloved people back. I love them so much and I have never stopped loving them.

There is so much I have planned for us together. It is mind blowing. They can't even comprehend what I have planned until they see me."

So, God sent His son with a vision, a mission, and values (VMV).

Vision

- Bring God's kingdom on earth (e.g., Mark 1:15). In the New Testament [NASB1995], the phrase "kingdom of God" appears 66 times, "kingdom of heaven" appears 32 times.

Mission

- Train (disciple) 12 men by example and teaching for three years (24 x 7) so they could continue His mission.

- Sentenced to death for crimes he never committed and killed. To pay the price so we never have to worry about it.

- Be resurrected.

Values

- "You shall love the Lord your God with all your heart, and with all your soul, and with all your mind" (Matthew 22:37, NASB1995).

- "You shall love your neighbor as yourself" (Matthew 22:39, NASB1995).

Jesus completed his mission never wavering from his vision and values. His disciples had the same vision and values, except their mission was different. Here was the apostles's VMV:

Vision

- Bring God's kingdom on earth (e.g., Mark 1:15). In the New Testament [New American Standard Bible (NASB) 1995], the phrase "kingdom of God" appears 66 times, "kingdom of heaven" appears 32 times.

Mission

- Have the courage to meet the demands of reality.

- Make disciples.

- Understanding God makes the decision of who will be the disciples.

Values

- "You shall love the Lord your God with all your heart, and with all your soul, and with all your mind" (Matthew 22:37, NASB1995).

- "You shall love your neighbor as yourself" (Matthew 22:39, NASB1995).

And our vision, mission, and values are the same as the apostles's VMV.

Vision

- Bring God's kingdom on earth (e.g., Mark 1:15). In the New Testament [NASB1995], the phrase "kingdom of God" appears 66 times, "kingdom of heaven" appears 32 times.

Mission

- Have the courage to meet the demands of reality.

- Make disciples.

- Understanding God makes the decision of who will be the disciples.

Values

- "You shall love the Lord your God with all your heart, and with all your soul, and with all your mind" (Matthew 22:37, NASB1995).

- "You shall love your neighbor as yourself" (Matthew 22:39, NASB1995).

Jesus expects us to follow Him. He fixed the problem. He brought us back to the Father. In the meantime, we are to be busy setting up the Kingdom. As we do this, the Holy Spirit transforms us into the likeness of Jesus. It is only when we are doing His work that we are being transformed.

Jack wasn't becoming a better pirate when he hung around other pirates. He became a better pirate when he figured out who he really was, helped others become better people. When his crew saw what a good pirate (person) he had become, someone they could really trust, they could not in their hearts leave him stranded. They had to come and rescue him. No one told them to. It wasn't out of fear. It was by his example of being a good man.

CHAPTER SEVENTEEN: MINDFULNESS, AWARENESS, AND PRESENCE

"Take what you can, give nothing back." (POTC1)
Are you making disciples?

"Take what you can, give nothing back." That was Jack's philosophy but certainly not the one of most pirates. In the world, God is thinking the same for us. We are in every situation for a reason and every time we have crossed paths with another person, it is for a reason. So, we need to "take what we can" so to speak. Be present. and mindful of the circumstances.

Perhaps we can help another person not just with a handout but by networking to get them in touch with the right people. And no, not just by sharing a phone number, but by personally making the introduction. It is going to use our time. Perhaps we are in the situation to better our own life. Someone has been placed there to help us. If we are not present to the situation and open, we just might miss it. "Take what you can, give nothing back." In that case you really had nothing to share. God is *always* working in all our lives, but if we are so caught up in tasks, success, deadlines, etc., we miss what God is trying to do for us and others. He will continue trying but it is so much easier on us all if we just catch it the first time. Gain those riches and move on to higher things. One can not imagine what is out there until he loses sight of what he knows. We are helping others do it while learning along the way. Recognizing when God sends us others to help us. The more we do this, the more we will know and recognize when someone is not sent by God. We will also know what is actually helping another to grow, not encouraging the other's disfunction to continue.

It may be possible to sense that little voice or push in your heart. Sense that nudge and realize this could be the Holy Spirit. Then as you pray, take time to listen. Several minutes, not seconds. It's like hearing a voice in your head. Over time the voice will always be the same. Jesus said, "My sheep listen to my voice." (John 10:22a, NIV1984). You will then learn when it's not his voice. This takes time. Years for some of us. Don't get discouraged. Praying is talking and listening. The more you talk and listen, the more your relationship grows, the more you trust. This happens a lot when I read the Bible, or listen to a sermon, or a speaker, or I am in a Bible study. All of a sudden, I will get a new insight. Inside my being I will know it is right. That is the Holy Spirit. Of course, I go back and check and sure enough it is right. It is usually not someone saying, "This is what this means"; it happens as I am listening to the speaker. The thought will come to me, "He is right. Before I always thought it meant such and such, but what it really meant was this."

Two things happened in my life that have helped me learn how to listen to God. One was in my 20s when I took a Bible study with Bible Study Fellowship. Growing up as a Roman Catholic, I was very unfamiliar with the Bible. The study was on Genesis. We met once a week, had a lecture, then met in a small group to share our answers and how they fit into our life from the previous week's homework. When you did your homework, you could only use your Bible. No commentary, no references, no outside help, just the Bible. Needless to say, the first few weeks didn't go well for me. As I would sit and ponder the questions, I would begin to hear that still, small voice. When I would pray, that same voice was there. At first this was very weird. It wasn't a voice I heard with my ears, but in my head. As the year progressed, I accepted that it must be the Holy Spirit. I also realized I was changing and slowly, very slowly, becoming more like

Jesus. I realized it not because I saw it, but because other people kept telling me that I was different. I had changed. My husband gave me a Bible because I did not own one and had to borrow one from the library. With his permission I'm sharing his inscription:

My Dearest Marty,

I have not written this sooner because I have been trying to think of a way to tell you how much I love you. I am writing this now not because I have solved the problem, but because I want you to have your Bible now. I have not included a quote from the Bible to assist you in your studies because I have not yet found a passage that has a particularly personal meaning. The importance of this Bible comes from the changes I have seen in you since you have been studying the Bible. While I haven't yet begun to study the Bible, it is your deep faith which has eliminated any doubts I had and made my faith in the Lord complete. I pray that this Bible will assist you in the study of our Lord and comfort you in times of need.

With Love and affection,

Your husband Dan

I will treasure this for as long as I live. I really hadn't noticed any changes in myself.

The other study that helped me was *Experiencing God*, by Henry T. Blackaby, Claude V. King, and Richard Blackaby. It was so reassuring to me. I do want to emphasize that God never tells you what other people should do. He is only interested in helping you conform to the likeness of his Son Jesus. He was always pointing out in my life things that needed to be changed. He did this in the most delicate way and only when I was ready to receive it. He also provided all the people and environment I would need to help me though the change. I just had to trust Him and hang in there. It was painful many times but so worth it. I will go into detail in my next book, *Look for the Miracles*.

CHAPTER EIGHTEEN:
ASKING FOR INSTRUCTIONS

"Do you think he plans this all out or just makes
it up as he goes along?" (POTC3)

Everyone is always so baffled by Jack. He manages to slip away from every dangerous situation. He always lands on top. It's like he knows what is going to happen before it does, and then has a plan to escape. But he really does not. He is always present to the moment and deals with the situation at hand. He does not fight it or wish and pray it were different. There is a great deal Jack could teach us about our life. When bad things come our way and things start to fall apart, we run to God, asking him to fix it or remove the pain. Rather, we should ask God "How do you want me to deal with this situation? God, I know You can do anything, even make it all go away, but what is best for me, and all the other people involved? Do You want them to partner with me in working out Your purpose for the Kingdom. How do You want me to handle this? What is my next move?" Praying this prayer takes real courage! Facing real demands as God wants.

But as I mentioned in the previous chapter, if you are living in the present and listening for direction, God wants what is best for you. God knows what He wants for the end result, but man has free will. He will not force anything, but if you say, "Here I am," He uses the present situation to make it happen. This takes a lifetime before we get it right. Fortunately

for us He is there every step of the way. Whatever we do not accomplish here we will continue in heaven. I do not believe when we die all we will do is sit around praising God and glorifying Him. I think the real praise and glory is about following His mission. God is always on the move. Likewise so will we be. We will get to see what He really had planned before the fall. And then as team members we will carry out that Mission.

CHAPTER NINETEEN:
SET SAIL.

"World's still the same, there's just less in it." (POTC3)
Christian pirates, that is.

Both Jack and Barbossa were walking away from the kraken, a creature that terrorized many. The kraken had a legacy known to every sailor, whether lad or missy, man, or woman. Each had their own picture of him in their mind. But now he was dead. There was no question what he looked like. Wasn't as big as many thought. Or as strong, as he lay there lifeless. Yes, at that moment the world seemed the same and they were grieving a great loss. Remember all those sci-fi movies with time travelers where they all could go back in time, but they could change nothing? For if they did the world wouldn't be what it is today.

I challenge you to put the book down, get some paper and a pen, and pick a year. It doesn't matter which one. Describe the year. Now, go back and describe the year without you in it. Not only did your family change, but your absence rippled out into the community, even the world in some cases.

If this is the case, be brave and take a chance. Break away and see what is in store for you. (No, I am not saying quit your job, sell everything, move to Africa, and join the missions or Peace Corps. But if that has been your life dream by all means…)

What ties are binding you?

Are you concerned with what family will think of you? Sorry, but when you leave home, you start the next family and just become a subset of theirs.

Is it work holding you back? Because all that is expected of you is to do what you were hired to do and do it with excellence. If that means you have to help others so you can get the job done, then do so. That's what Jack did with Will. Did he want to? By all means, no. But did it achieve what he needed? You bet. Did Will become an excellent sailor? Yes, and in some areas better than Jack. In fact, I wouldn't be surprised if Will taught Jack a few things.

There are no coincidences in this world. Not only are people placed in our path to help us grow, but we are placed in their path to help them grow. Once we can relax and be present in the moment, miracles do happen.

When Jack came face-to-face with the kraken he didn't run or panic. Was he scared out of his skin? You bet. But he had the courage to meet the demands of reality, all the while expecting a miracle. Did he die? No. Instead he was spat up on an island. So, try to look around at what has been given to you and listen to what HE is telling you. The more you listen, the more you will recognize His voice. Then do it.

The world is not supposed to stay the same. Our God is not stagnant. Yes, He is the same yesterday, today, and tomorrow. But he's in the business of reconciling all to a healthy relationship with Him.

The French writer André Gide warns us, "One does not discover new lands without consenting to lose sight of the shore for a very long time" (*Simple Abundance* February 24) So, set your sails, weigh anchor, cast off, and feel the wind at your back. Keep a weather eye and "go find that horizon!"

BE A PIRATE! The pirate God intended you to be, not the one where others tell you what you should be!